LIVING
IN THE IMAGE
OF CHRIST

The laity in ministry

LIVING IN THE IMAGE OF CHRIST

Hans-Ruedi Weber

WCC Publications, Geneva

This WCC edition published 1986 by special arrangement
with Judson Press, Valley Forge, PA, USA.

ISBN 2-8254-0870-0

© 1986 Judson Press, Valley Forge, PA, USA.

Cover design: Rob Lucas, The Netherlands

Cover photo: "Sower at sunset" by Vincent van Gogh, printed with
permission from Rijksmuseum Kröller-Müller, Otterlo, The Netherlands

Typeset in the USA

Printed in Switzerland

Contents

Introduction

Science fiction novels describe a time machine by which it is possible to travel forward and backward in time. While preparing the following studies for the congress on "The Laity in Ministry" (held at Andover Newton Theological School in the United States, in October 1985), I felt like sitting in such a time machine. Twenty-five years ago it had been my daily bread to read, write, and conduct seminars around the world on the ministry of the laity, but since then too many other matters have kept me busy.

During the 1950s and 1960s the ministry of the laity was indeed one of the most challenging subjects in the air. The basic scholarly study by Yves-M. Congar, *Jalons pour une théologie du laïcat* (Paris, 1953; English translation: London: Bloomsbury Pub. Co., 1957), and the appeal and manifesto by Hendrik Kraemer, *A Theology of the Laity* (London: Lutterworth Press, 1958), began to have their impact. Experiments and reflection groups on the ministry of the laity sprang up almost simultaneously in many parts of the world. The Department on the Laity of the World Council of Churches created links across denominational and continental frontiers between the various expressions of this exciting movement. Working for the Laity Department felt like surf-riding on a ground swell of modern church history.

However, church structures proved to be much more difficult to renew than we had expected. Christian obedience in the midst of the institutions of society leads to a much more precarious life than writers on the ministry of the laity then tended to assume. Remembering the former expectations, one is humbled by the small impact which the rediscovery of the laity has made on the churches and the world. Nevertheless, it is exhilarating to see a new generation at work, taking up the main insights of twenty-five years ago, learning from the mistakes then made, and experimenting with new ways to incarnate the vision of the church worshiping God and serving in the world.

The focal lectures of the Andover Newton Laity Congress were commissioned by the Boardman Lectureship, which prescribes that they address the following two questions: "How will you account for Jesus of Nazareth?" and "What will you do for Jesus?" Perhaps it would be more accurate to ask: "What will Jesus do for us and with us as we hear his call?" "What will Jesus do for and with the laity in ministry?" The term "laity" has always been problematic, and I believe that we have now come to a dead end with this designation (compare Note 1 of Chapter 1). When this term is used in the following pages, it simply designates men, women, and children who attempt to live as Christians both in the presence of God and in the midst of the world. Thus, the "ministry of the laity" concerns primarily the *human* vocation, lived in the light of Christ.

Three worldwide human quests will be taken up to examine how Christ responds to them:

The Human Search for Wisdom as we face the present threat of annihilation of creation—and the response of *Christ the sage*.

The Human Cry for Justice because of the oppressive impact of present economic and political structures—and what *Christ the crucified* teaches us in the struggle for justice.

The Human Need for Identity as many cultures and social groups experience a deep crisis of selfhood—and the way in which *Christ the artist* can restore God's image in us.

Most often Christ is perceived in the classical threefold way as prophet, priest, and king. These are good biblical keys for understanding the work of Christ, but they do not do justice to the much richer and far more diverse biblical testimonies to

Christ's ministry. To see Christ as the sage, the crucified, and the artist is avowedly a partial and one-sided approach which must be complemented by other biblical views of Christ. However, until now these aspects of Christ's ministry have been seldom explored in connection with the ministry of the laity. Therefore, they can throw some new light on the human vocation which we are called to live as followers of Christ.

A relatively large place will be given to insights gained from the Old Testament and the intertestamental literature. Jesus Christ must be seen against the background of Old Testament affirmations of God's action in creation and history. He must also be placed in the context of the Jewish milieu of his time. Studies on the ministry of the laity have too much neglected the Old Testament, though it is highly relevant for those who want to accomplish their human vocation in the light of Christ, whose "Bible" was the Hebrew Scriptures.

In the 1950s and 1960s the fourth chapter of Ephesians played an important role in the reflection on the ministry of the laity. This text has therefore been reexamined, and the transcription of a Bible study on it concludes the three studies.

It is not for a professional theologian to spell out in detail what the ministry of Christians means in various professions and institutions of today's society. Discerning God's will and discovering the concrete steps of obedience must be done by a common search by people living in similar professional and institutional milieus. However, corporate Bible study can play an important role in this process of discernment and be part of the nurturing for ministry. The focal lectures at Andover Newton were therefore not delivered in the form of monological "lectures" but as participatory Bible studies, using worksheets with the texts to be studied and questions for personal reflection and corporate discussion. Just as in the apostle Paul's time each of the Christians in Corinth had a lesson and interpretation to contribute, so today each one can enrich the corporate study by questions and insights.

November 1985   *H.R.W.*

1

The Human Search for Wisdom and Christ the Sage

How shall we focus on Christ in order to gain some new insights for the laity in ministry? Often too narrow a framework is chosen. We tend to start with the church and Christ's relation to it. The ministry of the laity[1] is then essentially seen within the framework of church activities, and all too soon we are entangled with questions of definition: Who are the laity as compared to the clergy? Is it biblically legitimate at all to use such terms as "laity" and "clergy"? How do lay people and set-apart ministers relate with one another as they participate in Christ's ministry? Is baptism the ordination for the laity in ministry, or should we establish special commissionings?

However important these questions may be, another approach will be chosen in these explorations, a much wider framework which the evangelist John suggests to us at the very beginning of his Gospel. When John focuses on Christ, he first relates him to God and to the universe. He reminds us that all things were created by the Logos, by God's Word and Wisdom which became incarnate in Christ. *All* things means the inanimate and the animate, *all* animals and people on this earth, the cosmos and the atom, the bread and the wine, the neighbor and the foreigner, the whole creation.

This is the world where most Christians live and work. John's way of focusing on Christ is therefore a good way for gaining insights about the laity in ministry. For this reason we start by recalling the biblical creation stories. They are not scientific descriptions of how the universe came into being. Rather, they are affirmations of faith, confessing who the Creator is and what our human vocation is to be on this earth.

Creation and Destruction

"In the beginning God created the heavens and the earth" (Genesis 1:1).[2] With solemn, liturgical language the priests wrote Genesis 1. They confess that out of chaos God created the cosmos. The powerful divine word called forth the order of heaven and earth, land and water, the seasons and the trees, the fish and the birds. This hymnic creed is punctuated by the recurring response "And there was evening and there was morning one [a second, third, fourth] day" until that crucial sixth day of creation when God made the animals on the dry land, together with human beings. The litany leads to a glorious climax when "God saw every thing that he had made, and behold, it was very good."

There is also a second, much older narrative account (2:4b–25) where God enlists the collaboration of the human beings for transforming the desert of the primal world into a beautiful garden. Adam and Eve are called upon to collaborate in the ongoing process of creation by tilling the ground, naming what was created, and giving birth to children, thus continuing the chain of generations.

The process of creation has indeed continued. Most of us no longer live in a garden but in a city, surrounded by things which have not naturally grown but are the work of human minds and hands, of machines and management. This is the world where the majority of Christians live and work. Theological reflection about creation stands, therefore, at the center of any theological reflection about the ministry of the laity. The primary *Christian* vocation is to accomplish responsibly our *human* vocation: to be partners of God in the ongoing work of creation.

In this task we have deeply failed. I will spare you an analysis of our present world situation. Instead let us listen to how an American singer perceived the human predicament of today in a poem called "Reverse Creation."

REVERSE CREATION

In the end, man was destroying his heaven, called earth. The earth was beautiful until man moved over it.

And man said, let there be darkness, and there was darkness. Man said the darkness was good and he called his darkness— security. And there was no evening and no morning on the seventh day before the end.

Then man said, let there be National governments to divide and control us in our darkness. Let there be leaders to lead us in our darkness so we may know our enemies. There was no morning on the sixth day before the end.

Then man said, let us create an army to control men's bodies and minds and let us extend our darkness all over the earth. Let us create rockets and bombs to kill faster and easier and at a distance for we must protect our security. And there was no morning on the fifth day before the end.

And then man said, let us travel to the moon and planets and stars for we must extend our security—while other men starve on earth we will reach for the stars—and there was no morning on the fourth day before the end.

Then man said, let us create escapes for ourselves. Let us have drugs and pep pills, goof balls, tranquilizers, advertisers, opiates, barbiturates, L.S.D., S.T.P., S.E.X., Compōz—for we are troubled by reality since it disturbs our security. And there was no morning on the third day before the end.

And then man said, let us create God in our own image lest some other god compete with us. Let us say God thinks as we think, hates as we hate, and kills as we kill. And there was no morning on the day before the end.

And on the last day there was a great noise on the face of the earth, and there was silence. The blackened earth rested to worship the one true God. And He saw all that man had done. And in the silence over the smouldering remains—He wept.[3]

In Search of Wisdom

Where do we go from here? Shall we close our eyes to reality and retire into a cozy individualist or otherworldy spirituality? Shall we join the apocalyptic messengers with their paralyzing announcement that world apocalypse is now? Shall we become prophets of judgment, unmasking and denouncing the powerful who have led us astray, the hidden persuaders of the mass media or—more honestly—the self-seeking greed in us all?

Another way to face the reality of our mismanagement of God's creation is the search for wisdom.[4] It is a deeply biblical way which has been too much disregarded. Large parts of the Bible are indeed wisdom literature, and Jesus not only knew this biblical tradition but also reaffirmed and reaccentuated it. Biblical wisdom progressed through three stages.

First, there was the old oral wisdom from the times before the Babylonian exile (i.e., before the sixth century B.C.). This wisdom has been gathered in several collections of proverbs (which are now found in Proverbs 10–31) and in many psalms. The preexilic wisdom has strongly marked the early redaction of the stories about David and Solomon. This wisdom also appears in the second narrative creation account, where the human beings are seen as partners in God's creation. Jesus was steeped in this old oral wisdom. He knew by heart many of the proverbs and psalms. The biblical creation stories and all that David did were Jesus' frame of reference. In fact, Jesus taught like the Jewish wisdom teachers, standing in the tradition of the great Israelite sages.

The second stage of biblical wisdom developed from the time of the Exile onward. We find it in postexilic psalms and the first nine chapters of the book of Proverbs. It expresses itself in the cries, the passionate questions, and the deep insights of Job as well as in the perceptive but sobering reflections of the book of Ecclesiastes. Also, intertestamental writings such as the Wisdom of Sirach and the Wisdom of Solomon continue this tradition, where wisdom is seen as a person, actively participating in God's creative work. Jesus certainly knew such postexilic wisdom speculations, and the early church saw in Christ this wisdom incarnate.

A final stage of biblical wisdom was reached with the death and resurrection of Christ. Most of the Old Testament traditions of faith were indeed taken up by Jesus. He not only incarnated them, but by his teaching, death, and resurrection reinterpreted them in a radical way. He did so also with the wisdom tradition. The apostle Paul, especially, has taught us what this radical wisdom of Christ means and what it implies for our Christian vocation.

We will examine on the basis of some biblical texts what each of the just mentioned stages of biblical wisdom can contribute to our reflection on the laity in ministry.

Trustees of the Universe

The old oral wisdom, the first stage, speaks about everyday life and everyday decisions, for instance on how to eat:

> Better is a dinner of herbs where love is
> than a fatted ox and hatred with it.
> —Proverbs 15:17

Such a simple truth can be extended to the whole of our life, for example:

> Better is a little with [justice]
> than great revenues with injustice.
> —16:8

There are many observations and good advice on how people are to live together as rich and poor, as young and old, as women and men, as friends and enemies:

> It is better to live in a corner of the housetop
> than in a house shared with a [nagging] woman [or man].
> —25:24

He who meddles in a quarrel not his own
    is like one who takes a passing dog by the ears.
                        —26:17

If your enemy is hungry, give him bread to eat;
    and if he is thirsty, give him water to drink;
for you will heap coals of fire on his head,
    and the LORD will reward you.
                        —25:21–22

The sages observed the facts of life as they really are, whether this observed reality pleased them or not. Thus, they saw what happened to the poor farmhands of the rich land-owners:

The fallow ground of the poor yields much food,
    but it is swept away through injustice.
                        —13:23

The Proverbs deal with this world, and only seldom does God appear. This has made the old biblical wisdom suspect to theologians and overpious believers. For Christians who spend most of their time in ordinary jobs of the everyday world, however, this wisdom rings a bell. Many of the old proverbs contain accumulated empirical knowledge and common sense, insights of generations of wise men and women who patiently observed and sorted out what leads to life and what leads to death. Why should we neglect this wisdom? There is still more to learn from Proverbs for a reflection on the laity in ministry.

Contrary to other biblical traditions of faith, the wisdom literature makes little distinction between Israelites and people of other faiths. Wisdom is not sectarian. The Old Testament sages learned from whatever source they could, be it Egyptian, Babylonian, or old Israelite insights. Seldom did they talk about election and salvation, for their primary concern was the penultimate questions of life here on earth, common to all human beings. This is a good antidote against much talk about the laity where one wants to find out exactly what distinguishes Christians from people of other faiths and ideologies.

Still more important is the observation that the Israelite

sages did not make decisions for those whom they counseled. The priests declared, "You shall!" and more often, "You shall not!" The prophets authoritatively announced, "Thus says the Lord!" The sages, however, simply put forward alternatives. They showed what probably leads to life and what almost certainly is a way to death. They knew that in this world we move in a gray area where compromises cannot be avoided, where seldom a totally good or totally bad decision can be reached. A proverb acknowledges this essential ambiguity of life:

> There is a way which seems right to a man,
> but its end is the way to death.
> —16:25

The sages, therefore, taught people to become mature so that they could make responsible decisions and act freely. One wonderful proverb not only shows how God wants us to search out things but also challenges us to act as kings:

> It is the glory of God to conceal things,
> but the glory of kings is to search things out.
> —25:2

The sages thus saw human beings as persons whom God trusts, to whom God gives freedom for making wise or foolish choices in the stewardship of their own lives and in their trusteeship over this earth. Again, this is a good antidote to much Christian preaching which so often gives the laity a chronically bad conscience. The message of the Old Testament sages is: "God trusts you! Decide and act, knowing that God has power to correct and to overrule your ambiguous and sometimes downright foolish choices."

At the heart of this biblical wisdom stands an affirmation of faith which the sages never tired to repeat:

"The fear [awe/trust] of the LORD is instruction in wisdom" (15:33).
"The fear [awe/trust] of the LORD is the beginning of wisdom" (9:10).

A person who is trusted by God and in turn puts his or her trust in God is truly free. Such men, women, and children are liberated from crippling fears and haunting anxieties of life. They confidently leave in God's hand the final outcome of their decisions and the ultimate destiny of this universe. They are free to act, from step to step, as David did. They are free to become God's partners in the act of creation, as the beginning of the second creation account suggests. When the earth and the heavens had been made, there still was no plant of the field, and no herb had yet sprung. Why? "For the LORD God had not caused it to rain upon the earth, and there was no [human being] to till the ground" (Genesis 2:5).

While speaking about the preexilic sages of Israel, one is constantly reminded of Jesus, the wisdom teacher, of Christ the great sage. In his parables he used events from ordinary life to teach us the secrets of God's kingdom. When eating with unclean tax collectors and speaking with the Samaritan woman, he broke through the taboos of Pharisaic exclusiveness. Above all, like the sages, he left us free to say "yes" or "no," to choose which way to go when faced with crucial alternatives. Matthew, especially, showed him as such a wisdom teacher. In the Sermon on the Mount Jesus challenged us: "Will you go through the wide or the narrow door? Do you build your house on sand or on stone?" (See 7:13-14, 24-27.) Later, in parables which only Matthew reports, put before us is the choice to act either as wise or foolish virgins and to be among the sheep or the goats. (See 25:1-13, 31-46.) Despite the disciples' and our own unbelief, he entrusted to them and entrusts to us his mission to the ends of the earth and the end of time. Jesus was *par excellence* the one who put his trust in God and who worked together with God. He did not force Jerusalem to repent. No fire fell on that city as it fell on Sodom and Gomorrah. As God wept over the destroyed creation in the poem presented earlier, so Jesus wept over Jerusalem.

Dame Wisdom

Jesus' weeping over Jerusalem brings us to the second stage of the biblical wisdom literature. There is, alas, no time to lis-

ten to Job, that great fighter with God who rejected the shallow
counsel and wisdom of his friends. Nor can we sit at the feet of
the preacher called Ecclesiastes who dared to see and say things
as they really are, unmasking the vanity of most human pur-
suits and calling in question the somewhat naive optimism of
the preexilic sages. We will look only at some passages which
portray wisdom as a person and explore what such postexilic
wisdom speculations might teach us about the laity in ministry.

In the theological introduction to the old collections of proverbs the personified Wisdom says:

> The LORD created me at the beginning of his work,
>   the first of his acts of old. . . .
> When he established the heavens, I was there. . . .
>   I was beside him, like a master workman
>   [or like a little child];
> and I was daily his delight,
>   rejoicing before him always.
> —Proverbs 8:22–30

The link between wisdom and God's creating work is clearly
expressed in this passage, but the identity of wisdom does not
yet become clear. Is wisdom the architect who collaborates
with God or the little child who accompanies God's creative
activity with rejoicing? Both translations are possible, but as
the passage continues, wisdom reveals herself as a hostess, as
Dame Wisdom. The Old Testament terms for wisdom are
indeed feminine: *chokma* in Hebrew and *sophia* in Greek.
Dame Wisdom has built her house, prepared a feast, and now
invites all those who are simple-minded to come to her and
learn from her.

This learning community into which Dame Wisdom invites
us is described in the language of love. In the book of Sirach the
following description is given:

> The man who fears the Lord will do this. . . .
> [Wisdom] will come to meet him like a mother,

and like the wife of his youth she will welcome him.
She will feed him with the bread of understanding
     and give him the water of wisdom to drink.
He will lean on her and will not fall,
     and he will rely on her and will not be put to shame.
She will exalt him above his neighbors,
     and will open his mouth in the midst of the assembly.
                                              —Sirach 15:1–5

The beautiful hymn to wisdom found in another intertestamental book exalts wisdom as "the fashioner of all things." It is
revealing to compare this creation hymn with the two creation
stories of Genesis, for one can detect in wisdom's way of creating quite a different style and manner of work from that
described in the first two chapters of the Bible. Wisdom is "the
fashioner of all things."

For wisdom is more mobile than any motion;
because of her pureness she pervades and penetrates all things.
For she is a breath of the power of God,
and a pure emanation of the glory of the Almighty. . . .
. . . she is a reflection of eternal light,
a spotless mirror of the working of God,
and an image of his goodness . . .
. . . while remaining in herself, she renews all things;
in every generation she passes into holy souls
and makes them friends of God, and prophets . . .
. . . she is more beautiful than the sun.
                                    —Wisdom of Solomon 7:24–29

The writer of this hymn then confesses:

I loved her and sought her from my youth,
and I desired to take her for my bride,
and I became enamoured of her beauty.
She glorifies her noble birth by living with God,
and the Lord of all loves her.
For she is an initiate in the knowledge of God,
and an associate in his works.
                                              —8:2–4

The Scottish theologian Rosemary Houghton has made an
interesting analysis of the creation stories in Genesis and the

creative activity of Dame Wisdom.[5] In the Genesis chapters she perceives God as creating the universe in a typical "masculine" way, i.e., working from the outside. By a commanding word God separates the elements and brings order into the chaos. Out of dust God models man and puts him in the garden to till the ground. In contrast to this, Dame Wisdom works not by separation and decrees; God's creative power is perceived here as shaping things in a more "feminine" manner: Wisdom seeks communion. She pervades and penetrates all things. She renews the creation by a loving relationship, by changing the earth and human persons from within, so that light and friendship and beauty appear.

Perhaps the just mentioned analysis of two different ways of creating uses too strong stereotypes of what is considered to be typically "masculine" and "feminine," but Rosemary Houghton never goes to the point of speaking of a male or female God. She simply observes that in Genesis God's way of work is perceived as more masculine, while in the Book of Sirach and the Wisdom of Solomon a more feminine way of work can be detected. Both ways are, according to her, biblical and complement each other. It is certainly true, however, that the more masculine way has predominated.

The writer of the song "Reverse Creation" with which this exploration began must have consciously used the term "man." It is a typically masculine way to divide humanity into races, religions, and classes, to build governments and armies, and to set nation against nation. This way finally destroys the earth. Could it be that in our stewardship over the earth all of us, both men and women, have acted in a too one-sidedly masculine way? Is this at least one of the reasons why we have pollution, social and political tension, and a suicidal armament race to the degree we do today? Even in our reflections about the laity in ministry we may have thought too exclusively about lay*men* only.[6] It would be interesting to analyze from this point of view what in the 1950s and 1960s was written about work and vocation. My guess is that much was reasoned then from a very one-sidely masculine perspective. Up to 1955 the World Council of Churches published a bulletin called *Laymen's Work*, which later continued with the more general title *Laity*. In 1963 Stephen Neill and I edited a large volume in which we attempted to rewrite church history not as the story of clerics and ecclesiastical institutions but from the point of view of Christians being present in the struggles and institutions of society. In that volume women were seen to play a very important role, but the book was entitled *The LayMAN in Christian History* (emphasis added). Nobody protested then, but today such a title would be impossible.

This turn from sexist language indicates an important new trend. There is indeed no doubt that during the last few decades the greatest advance with regard to the laity in ministry was the growth of women's movements. In questions of justice and peace and in the struggle for safeguarding the integrity of creation, some of the most important challenges and insights have come from women. I hope, therefore, that women will continue to work hard on the questions: What is a truly feminine way of participating in God's creative work? What can Dame Wisdom teach both men and women for our vocation to be trustees of this universe?

While listening to the postexilic passages about the personified Wisdom, many will have been reminded of the beginning of John's Gospel. This Johannine prologue has an interesting parallel in the intertestamental book of Sirach where Wisdom proclaims:

> "I came forth from the mouth of the Most High,
>   and covered the earth like a mist.
> I dwelt in high places,
>   and my throne was in a pillar of cloud.
> Alone I have made the circuit of the vault of heaven
>   and have walked in the depths of the abyss. . . .
> and in every people and nation I have gotten a possession."
> —Sirach 24:2–6

But then this all-pervading Wisdom seeks a resting place to put up her tent, a place where she could take root and grow like a cedar. She found that place on Mount Zion in Jerusalem, and the hymn leads up to the affirmation:

> All this is the book of the covenant of the Most High God,
> the law which Moses commanded us. . . .

—24:23

There are so many parallels between this passage and the beginning of John's Gospel that some scholars wonder whether that hymn of Wisdom did not serve as a model for John's prologue. However, while for Sirach, Wisdom finally is seen "incarnate" in the Torah, the Jewish Law, John testifies that God's Word and Wisdom became incarnate in Jesus Christ.

The early Christians indeed recognized in Christ's attitudes and sensibility the characteristic traits of the personified Wisdom. No doubt, Jesus was a man, sometimes showing forth strong masculine ways of action. But he did not suppress the more feminine perceptions of life which are dormant in all human beings. Through his fully developed humanity Christ the sage, the Wisdom incarnate, can teach us much about the laity in ministry. For in this ministry we need to develop all human potentialities, both the more masculine and the more feminine sensibilities.

The Wisdom of the Cross

The final stage of biblical wisdom was reached when Jesus went the way to Golgotha to die on the cross. In a crucial conversation near Caesarea Philippi, when the hour of truth came near, Jesus said: "Whoever would save his life will lose it; and whoever loses his life for my sake and the gospel's will save it" (Mark 8:35). As a good wisdom teacher, Jesus put an alternative before his disciples, a difficult alternative about the ultimate outcome and meaning of our life. Even today all Christians have to face this alternative.

Trusting in God's will, though at that time not understanding it, Jesus made a choice and was ready to lay down his life. This led to that dark hour when on the cross he felt abandoned and let down: "My God, my God, why have you forsaken me?" (see Matthew 27:46). All seemed lost, and the Jesus story had come to a miserable end.

Things were turned upside-down. The disciples at first did not perceive it. All had fled. Two went home, deeply disappointed. The cross simply made no sense to them. Even when they received the firm conviction that Christ had risen from the dead, they could not understand why their Lord had to die. Only gradually, by looking at the crucifixion in the light of what they remembered of Jesus' words and acts and in the light of reinterpreted Old Testament texts did they discover the manifold meanings of Christ's Passion.

The apostle Paul became the first great theologian of the cross, and in his letters one finds several understandings of what Christ's Passion really meant. In one of his interpretations the cross is related to the human search for wisdom. He wrote to the Corinthians who had boasted to be strong and wise:

> The word of the cross is folly to those who are perishing, but to us who are being saved it is the power of God. For it is written,
>
> > "I will destroy the wisdom of the wise,
> > and the cleverness of the clever I will thwart."
> > —Isaiah 29:14
>
> Where is the wise man? Where is the scribe? Where is the debater of this age? Has not God made foolish the wisdom of the world? For since, in the wisdom of God, the world did not know God through wisdom, it pleased God through the folly of what we preach to save those who believe. For Jews demand signs and Greeks seek wisdom, but we preach Christ crucified, a stumbling block to Jews and folly to Gentiles, but to those who are called, both Jews and Greeks, Christ the power of God and the wisdom of God (1 Corinthians 1:18–24).

Paul did not deny that through human wisdom the world could have known God. One might add that through learning wisdom we could indeed become responsible trustees of the universe. But reality in Paul's time and ours proves that our foolishness perverts such possible knowledge of God and such responsible trusteeship over creation. We make and serve idols instead of standing in awe before the Creator. We foolishly exploit the earth and one another instead of participating in God's creative work.

A radical remedy, therefore, had to be applied which—according to human wisdom—is sheer folly. The vicious circle of greed and exploitation, of national security and the destruction of our earth, can be broken through only by the cross, the free giving of one's life for the life of the world.

In Paul's thinking the cross, therefore, became the ultimate wisdom. He could no more proclaim Christ except as the crucified one. The crucifixion was, so to say, Paul's spectacles through which the true reality of things could be perceived the way God perceives them. Expressed in more theological language, one can say that for Paul the crucifixion of Jesus became the hermeneutical key, i.e., the key for interpreting what really happens on the scene of our lives and of world history. The cross, the giving of one's life, is thus seen as the criterion for making ultimately wise or foolish decisions.

In quite another context, in the letter to the Galatians, which was written at about the same time as the first letter to the Corinthians, Paul summed up this new insight in a stenographic form: "Far be it from me to glory except in the cross of our Lord Jesus Christ, by which the world has been crucified to me, and I to the world" (Galatians 6:14). No new creation was thus conceivable for Paul except by way of the cross.

Can Christians in business, politics, their work, families, and neighborhoods really live with such a radical wisdom of the cross? Is it true that ultimately we can perceive the reality of this world only through the spectacles of the cross? Can we in our own lives verify Paul's claim that the crucifixion of Jesus gives us the criterion for making ultimately wise or foolish decisions? Such questions—and they are not rhetorical ones—cannot be answered through lectures and studies, but only in a life-long *praxis pietatis*, a practice of Christian discipleship.

In conclusion, we should remember that the last word does not devalue the words spoken beforehand. What is ultimately true, namely, the wisdom of the cross, does not annul what we learned as penultimate wisdom.

—Jesus, the wisdom teacher, did not despise the down-to-earth and common-sense wisdom of the preexilic sages. What they taught and what Jesus reaffirmed can still guide us in our Christian ministry.

—Jesus, the wisdom incarnate, lived what in postexilic times was testified about Dame Wisdom. Especially for a wise trust-eeship over this earth, we desperately need to correct too one-sidely masculine ways of work by more feminine sensibilities and approaches.

—However, there are moments in our lives and hours in history when nothing less than the wisdom of the cross will be sufficient to fulfill our ministry, when Christ the sage will be recognized as Christ the crucified.

2

The Human Cry for Justice and Christ the Crucified

In focusing our attention on Christ the sage, we came face to face with Jesus the crucified. In search of wisdom we were led to the folly of the cross. Personally I would like to move on now to the victory of the resurrection: to the new creation, the image of God which we see in Christ, who—like an artist—can restore God's image in us. The third lecture will concentrate on Christ the artist who gives us our true identity as human beings. However, in biblical faith there is no detour around the cross. Reflection about Christ's crucifixion must therefore remain a central part of our reflection on the laity in ministry.[1] What does the cross mean for Christian discipleship in a world where one can no longer remain deaf to the cry of millions of children, women, and men for justice?

Throughout this exploration an artwork, the crucifixion print by little-known German artist Georg Lemke, will accompany us. We understand not only through texts and analysis but also through images and meditation. Before proceeding it is therefore good to let, in silence, Lemke's print speak to us.[2]

The Harsh Reality of Crucifixion

What did actually happen on that ominous Friday, probably April 7 of the year A.D. 30, just outside the first-century walls of Jerusalem? For the historians of that time it was simply a miscellaneous event, the routine execution of one more Jewish fanatic and rebel. Most Greek and Latin historians do not even mention it. At the beginning of the second century Tacitus makes a short side remark about Christ's death in his *Annals of Imperial Rome*. Reporting about Nero who used the Christians as scapegoats, he comments that "the pernicious superstition" of Christianity derived its name from a certain "Christus, who, in the reign of Tiberius, was condemned to death by the procurator Pontius Pilate" (XV,44). Towards the end of the first century the Jewish historian Flavius Josephus wrote in twenty volumes *The Antiquities of the Jews*. There he reported a series of Jewish uproars provoked by Pilate, and in this connection Josephus mentions Jesus, "a wise man" and "teacher." He says that "on the indictment of the principal men among us, Pilate had condemned him to the cross" (XVIII, 3.3). This is about all the extra-biblical evidence we have on Christ's crucifixion.

More is known about the way in which crucifixions were actually conducted. Probably this way of execution was invented by the Persians and later widely used in the Roman Empire to punish revolting slaves, deserters, and especially the Jewish rebels in Palestine. The torture was so cruel that Roman law forbade its infliction upon Roman citizens. Having been flogged, those who were to be crucified had to carry the crossbar to the place of execution where the cross poles stood already firmly fixed in the ground. With their wrists bound or nailed on the crossbar the victims were pulled up to the top or to an indentation on the upper part of the cross pole. This pole also had a *sedile*, a peg of wood sticking out, on which those to be executed were seated, so that they could continue to breathe. Finally the executioners nailed or bound the feet of the victims on the cross pole which had no foot rest as is wrongly portrayed in most Christian art. Thus "sitting on the cross" the victims could stay alive through cold nights and hot days as long as they had the strength to keep themselves upright and breathe. This struggle could last for several days, until the victims gradually died of asphyxiation. Josephus tells us about mass crucifixions of this kind in the period before and during the first Jewish war, where hundreds of Jewish rebels were thus seated on crosses.

The harshness of crucifixion suddenly came home to many Jews and Christians when in 1968 for the first time the remnants of a crucified man from the time of Jesus were found in an ossuary near Jerusalem. We even know his name, which is written on the coffin: Jehohanan ben Hagqol. The following sketch shows how, on the basis of the remains found, archeologists could reconstruct the probable position of Jehohanan on the cross. According to the skull and certain deformations of it even the facial expressions of this crucified man could be reestablished.[3]

Why is it that Jehohanan ben Hagqol and the many thousands of other Jews who were crucified in Palestine have been forgotten, while the agony of Jesus became very central in Christian faith and worship? Why did the early Christians and the Gospel writers not conceal this ignominious and scandalous death of their Lord? Contrary to what one might expect, in the early Christian creeds Christ's death is almost always mentioned. The Passion story was probably the first large cycle of "Jesus stories" fixed in the oral tradition, later to be incorporated in all four Gospels of the New Testament.

From Bare Facts to Deep Meanings

Soon after the crucifixion, first some women and then the disciples received the firm conviction that Jesus was alive. They had met him and seen visions of him. True, Jesus had died on the cross and had been buried, but now he was risen from the tomb and present with them. Without this mysterious event of the resurrection, the crucifixion of Jesus would have remained a series of dumb, bare facts without meaning.

The experience of the two disciples of Emmaus is like a parable for what happened among early Christians: These two followers of Christ went home with their hopes broken. Telling about the crucifixion of Jesus, they said to the stranger who joined them: "We had hoped that [Jesus] was the one to redeem Israel," but "it is now the third day since this happened" (see

Luke 24:19–21). This stranger was none other than the risen Lord, walking along with them. He opened their minds by interpreting for them the Scriptures in such a way that they could reread the books of Moses, the prophets, and the Psalms in the light of what Jesus had taught, in the light of his death and resurrection (vv. 26–27; compare vv. 44–49). Later, at table with them "he took the bread and blessed, and broke it, and gave it to them" (v. 30). This series of gestures opened the eyes of the disciples of Emmaus, because they remembered the same gestures from the Last Supper. It was indeed during the early Christian worship where the believers recalled and meditated on the words and gestures of Jesus. In this way gradually they began to grasp something of the deep meanings of the crucifixion. This led them back to the study of the Jewish Scriptures, which they reread and found keys for understanding the scandal of the cross.

We saw already how the apostle Paul, the first great theologian of the cross, once interpreted Jesus' crucifixion as the paradoxical wisdom of God, as the key for the right kind of knowledge. Two or three decades later the orally transmitted Passion stories were fixed by writing. As each of the Four Evangelists gave his own interpretive account of the crucifixion, differently accentuated understandings of the death of Christ appeared. These were not simply theological creations of Gospel writers. Already in the stage of the oral tradition different perceptions of the meaning of the cross had developed.

The accompanying schematic drawing shows how this development from the bare facts of the crucifixion to the unfolding of its varied and deep meanings may have happened in the mind of the early church. The harsh facts were not concealed. Even when the early Christians could not yet grasp any meaning in the crucifixion, they nevertheless knew that the death of Christ had deep significance. Therefore, they preserved and transmitted what they had heard from eyewitnesses, for instance, Simon of Cyrene and the women who had been looking from afar. Such eyewitness reports are taken and woven differently into the interpretative crucifixion accounts

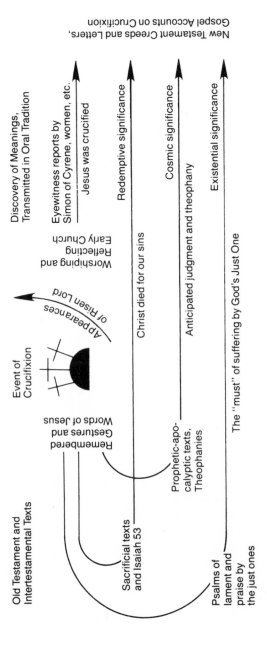

of the Four Evangelists. One only can guess what belonged to this recorded memory of the event. My own guess is that eye-witness reports may have included the carrying of the crossbar by Simon of Cyrene, the place of the execution called Golgo-tha, the crucifixion of two Jewish rebels together with Jesus, and inscription on the cross, the fact that Jesus actually died on the cross, the loud cry when he died, and perhaps an amazed exclamation of the Roman centurion; possibly other details mentioned in the crucifixion accounts came from eyewit-nesses.

Besides such factual remembrances, at least three different early strands of interpretative understandings of Christ's death can be detected behind the written documents of the New Tes-tament.

The Redemptive Significance: Christ Died for Our Sins

A very old interpretative tradition shows the redemptive sig-nificance of the crucifixion which links the cross with our sal-vation. The remembered words and gestures of the Last Supper played an important role in the formation of this tradi-tion. When the apostle Paul received the tradition, it had already become a creedal formula. He transmitted it to the Christians in Corinth when he stayed in that city in the early fifties: "I delivered to you as of first importance what I also received, that Christ *died for our sins* in accordance with the scriptures . . ." (1 Corinthians 15:3-5, emphasis added). No specific passage from the Scriptures is quoted. The scriptural bases for this first theological understanding were probably Old Testament texts about the atoning sacrifices as well as parts of the famous song of the suffering servant in Isaiah 53, which was now reinterpreted and applied to Jesus' life, death, and resurrection. This redemptive significance of Christ's death became central in Paul's theology, especially as it finds expression in his letter to the Galatians and the subsequent let-ter to the Romans. Because Christ died for our sins, because he suffered vicariously for us, we are liberated from guilt. Christ became what we are so that we may become what he is. By grace we are justified, set right before God. The apostle Paul stated this in the following way:

> While we were still weak, at the right time Christ died for the ungodly. Why, one will hardly die for a righteous man—though perhaps for a good man one will dare even to die. But God shows his love for us in that while we were yet sinners Christ died for us. Since, therefore, we are now justified by his blood, much more shall we be saved by him from the wrath of God. For if while we were enemies we were reconciled to God by the death of his Son, much more, now that we are reconciled, shall we be saved by his life (Romans 5:6–10).

This redemptive meaning of Christ's death has deep implications for the laity in ministry. How can we live our daily lives with that glorious freedom of forgiven sinners who need no more indulge in guilt complexes and morbid self-analysis? What does it mean for our presence in a society where one must constantly build up one's image and ego because that society judges people by their works, their achievements, because it is a society which lives by merit and not by grace? How does our justification by grace relate to our life in a world where we can no longer remain deaf to the cries for justice among the oppressed?

In Georg Lemke's crucifixion print we see this redemptive significance of Christ's death expressed by the one who from the cross bends down to the naked person in the grips of evil powers. Those who are being saved have nothing to offer, except empty hands and their face turned up to Christ. They are still captured by the idols of this world, but Christ died for the ungodly. Therefore, Christians can no longer have a conceited attitude to persons and groups who are weak and who out of darkness cry for help.

These are important implications for the ministry of the laity, but we will not further pursue them. The redemptive meaning of the cross and its significance for a truly Christian life have in all churches been strongly emphasized. There is therefore a wealth of good material for those who want to explore further what it means that Christ died for our sins. In fact, that particular significance of the crucifixion has become so dominant in the worship and in Christian education that other equally important theological meanings of the cross are being ignored.

The Cosmic Significance: God's Action in World History

A second very old interpretative tradition sees in the crucifixion of Jesus a cosmic event. What happened at the cross is perceived as an anticipated final judgment. Far from being merely a miscellaneous incident, a routine execution in a borderland of the Roman Empire, the crucifixion of Jesus is here understood as the decisive turning point of world history.

In Mark 15:20–41, probably the oldest written account of the crucifixion, the following signs point to this cosmic significance. First, the progression of events is emphasized in a *three-hour scheme;* at the third hour (that is, nine o'clock) is the actual crucifixion; at the sixth hour (that is, twelve o'clock) the darkness begins; finally, at the ninth hour (that is, three o'clock p.m.) come the loud cry and the death of Jesus (vv. 25, 33, 34, 37). Both in the Old Testament and intertestamental apocalyptic literature the events of the last days are often punctuated by such a sequence of fixed hours. Second, "there was *darkness* over the whole land" from the sixth until the ninth hour (v. 33, emphasis added). This darkness is especially significant. Such symbolic phenomena usually have several meanings. It may be that the early Christians saw in this darkness a sign of judgment about which the Old Testament prophets spoke (e.g., Amos 8:9; Joel 2:1–2). Darkness also recalls the first day of creation, when "darkness was upon the face of the deep" (Genesis 1:2); the death of Jesus at the ninth hour, when the darkness ended and the light returned, can thus point to the beginning of the new creation. Darkness is further mentioned in the Exodus story where Moses was ordered by God: "Stretch out your hand toward heaven that there may be darkness over the land of Egypt, a darkness to be felt" (Exodus 10:21–23); if the early Christians related the darkness of the cross with this passage from Exodus, then they saw in Christ's crucifixion a new exodus, a liberation from dark forces. Third, besides the signs of the hours and of the darkness, the mention of *the coming of Elijah* is significant, for the return of this prophet was intimately linked with the messianic times: "Behold, I will send you Elijah the prophet before the great and terrible day of the Lord comes" (Malachi 4:5–6). Fourth, *the rending of the temple curtain* is a powerful sign, although the exegetes have given it very different interpretations and we cannot know for certain exactly what it meant for the early Christians.

This old cosmic interpretation of the death of Christ was taken up and expanded by several New Testament authors. The evangelist Matthew has strongly emphasized it. Besides the few cosmic phenomena mentioned by Mark and Luke, he added in connection with the crucifixion the signs of the earthquake, the splitting of the rocks, the opening of the tombs, and the raising of some of the saints (Matthew 27:51–52). Such signs appear also in Old Testament accounts of theophanies (manifestations of God's presence), especially in the Moses/Sinai stories. Matthew describes thus the death of Jesus as a decisive theophany in response to the obedience unto death by Jesus, the Son of God. A quite different development of the same early Christian cosmic understanding of Christ's death is given by the visionary in the book of Revelation. There the cosmic repercussions of Golgotha are vividly portrayed.

It is a pity that this second early Christian understanding of the crucifixion, the cosmic interpretation, was much neglected in the worship and teaching of Western churches. This is one reason why Christian faith has for many church members become such a limited private affair, relating to questions of individual ethics only. Christian faith is then thought to be relevant for some rules of good conduct in business and banking but not for critically rethinking and changing the whole system of economy. It concentrates on interpersonal relationships in families, neighborhoods, and work places, but not on the power structures of society. The widespread overemphasis on the redemptive significance of Christ's death for our sins and the corresponding neglect of the cosmic significance of the cross have led to a dangerous dichotomy: we tend to be interested more in our justification by faith than in the justice of God. This dichotomy has even entered the Bible translations in many languages, where a distinction is made between "justice" and "righteousness." In the biblical languages only one word is used—zedaka in Hebrew and dikaiosyne in Greek. Most English translations render, for instance, Jesus' basic challenge in the Sermon on the Mount "Seek first God's kingdom and his righteousness!" This means exactly the same as: "Seek first God's kingdom and his justice!" (Matthew 6:33). In a world where millions of oppressed cry out for justice, this second translation has quite other connotations than the one speaking about righteousness. With the crucifixion of Jesus the powers of God's kingdom and God's justice have irrupted into world history, shaking the status quo of our societies and of the cosmos.

What does such a cosmic understanding of the cross mean for the laity in ministry? Many days would be needed to explore this, and only one of the many implications will be mentioned here: If Christ's crucifixion has indeed that world-shaking significance, then our whole outlook on history will change. We can then no longer live with the naive assumptions of the epoch of Enlightenment, though most Europeans and Americans are deeply marked by these beliefs of the Enlightenment: namely, that there will be gradual progress, that despite periodic drawbacks things will become better and better on this earth. Conversely, we cannot join with the apocalyptic doomsayers of our time. True, catastrophes will come, but within and beyond even cosmic catastrophes we can hold on to the assurance that the decisive victory has been won at the cross. Therefore we need not become victims of resignation, as we hear the cries of those who are oppressed. These cries echo the loud cry of Jesus the crucified when he overcame the forces of darkness.

In Georg Lemke's print the forces of darkness are present in a frightening way, revealing the overpowering threat to a vulnerable human being by the ancient idols and the modern mechanized and computerized world. However, when in the midst of day the night came, God was present. When in their blindness the evil powers thought that by crucifying the Christ they would win their victory, in fact they were defeated through the cross (1 Corinthians 2:8; Colossians 2:15). By his death Christ overpowered and submitted the one who has power of death (Hebrews 2:14).

The Existential Significance: Christ the Suffering Just One

A third early Christian understanding of the crucifixion emphasizes the divine "must" of Christ's suffering, the inherent necessity of his agony, exactly because Jesus was the Just One. This existential significance of the cross has also been much neglected in the worship and teaching of most churches. It was perhaps the oldest insight gained by the Christian believers who after the resurrection attempted to discover meaning in the incomprehensible event of crucifixion.

This third theological interpretation emphasizes the two trials of Jesus before the Jewish and the Roman authorities and the subsequent condemnation, agony and execution. In the crucifixion accounts especially there are many indications which relate the destiny of Jesus with the destiny of a figure who in the centuries before Christ began to play an important role in Jewish spirituality, namely, that of the suffering Just One. This Just One appears in a group of psalms which all begin with laments and often end with confidence and praise. The following list shows that these psalms are several times quoted or alluded to in the crucifixion accounts. Details of what Jesus had to suffer and what he said on the cross were also experienced and said by the psalmists.

Psalm 22:18—"They divide my garments among them, and for my raiment they cast lots." This scene of the division of garments is reported by all four Evangelists (Matthew 27:35; Mark 15:24; Luke 23:34; John 19:23–24).

Psalm 22:7—"All who see me mock at me, . . . they wag their heads." Such mocking and deriding, wagging of the heads, is mentioned by Mark and Matthew (Matthew 27:39, 41; Mark 15:29).

Psalm 22:8—"He committed his cause to the Lord; let him deliver him." According to Matthew (27:43), the chief priests and elders said almost the same to Jesus on the cross.

Psalm 22:1—"My God, my God, why hast thou forsaken me?" This cry is reported by the first two Evangelists. Matthew uses the Hebrew 'Eli' while Mark quotes the Aramaic 'Eloi' for the call "my God" (Matthew 27:46; Mark 15:34).

Psalm 69:21—"They gave me poison for food, and for my thirst they gave me vinegar to drink." Matthew mentions the poison, or gall, and all four Evangelists report the scene with someone bringing a sponge filled with vinegar to Jesus (Matthew 27:34, 48; Mark 15:36; Luke 23:36; John 19:28-29).

Psalm 22:15; 69:21—"My tongue cleaves to my jaws" and "For my thirst they gave me vinegar." According to John (19:28), Jesus said "(to fulfill the Scripture) 'I thirst!' " which probably recalls these passages from the Psalms.

Psalm 31:5—"Into thy hand I commit my spirit." According to Luke (23:46), Jesus died with this prayer from the psalm which is part of the Jewish evening prayers.

Psalm 38:11—"My friends and companions stand aloof from my plagues, and my kinsmen stand afar off." According to the first three Evangelists, the disciples had fled before the crucifixion, and the women who had followed Jesus (Luke adds: "and all his acquaintances") were looking from afar (Matthew 27:55; Mark 15:40; Luke 23:49).

Isaiah 53:12c—"He . . . was numbered with the transgressors." This quotation from the song of the suffering servant appears in some late manuscripts of Mark's crucifixion account (15:28, a verse which is rightly omitted in many modern translations or appears only as a footnote). Luke used the same quotation earlier in Jesus' final words to his disciples during the Last Supper (22:37). It is significant that the only explicit quotation of Isaiah 53 in the Passion stories does *not* refer to the vicarious suffering of God's servant for our sins. (Such vicarious suffering is indeed several times mentioned in Isaiah 53 [e.g., Isaiah 53:4–5, 6b, 10b, 11b, 12b, 12d].) In the verse quoted by Luke, God's Servant is portrayed as God's Just One who must suffer, probably also as the suffering prophet, but not as the vicariously suffering Servant (compare also Isaiah 53:7–10a, 11b).

This enumeration of striking correspondences between the crucifixion accounts in the Gospels and some isolated texts from the Psalms must not be understood as if the Evangelists had freely added all the details mentioned. Several of these details, especially the mocking and the dividing of Jesus' clothes, may well have been transmitted in the earlier mentioned eyewitness reports. However, the first Christians saw a profound analogy of situation between the destiny of Jesus and the destiny of the Just One who must suffer because he is just. Therefore, Christ's crucifixion was told with words and images from Psalm 22 and similar expressions of lament and confidence found in other psalms, some of the prophets, and intertestamental literature.

Those who are just, that is, those who trust God and walk according to God's command, will in this earthly life still receive their due reward. Such was the assumption of many Israelites before the Exile. However, life experience showed that it was the just ones who had much to suffer because they put their trust in God and made God's justice their cause. Therefore, we find many laments in the book of Psalms, like the moving beginning of Psalm 13:

> How long, O LORD? Wilt thou forget me for ever?
> How long wilt thou hide thy face from me?

Nevertheless, most of these laments end with a song of praise because those who prayed them were actually delivered out of their agony or received the firm conviction and hope that

somehow, sometime—perhaps even after their death—God
would vindicate them.

> When the [just] cry for help, the LORD hears,
> and delivers them out of all their troubles.
>   —34:17

Gradually it was thus seen that those who make God's justice their cause must suffer, but ultimately the Lord will vindicate and exalt them. A whole spirituality of God's just ones
developed. They knew that they had to suffer for the sake of
justice.

The most remarkable document of this spirituality is found
in the Wisdom of Solomon, a Jewish-Hellenistic writing from
the first century B.C. Like a diptych the suffering and the exaltation of the just one are set one over against the other. Both
the humiliation and the vindication of the just one are seen
through the eyes and minds of proud and cunning enemies of
God's justice, who then come under God's judgment.

Suffering of the just one (Wisdom 2:12-20)

"Let us lie in wait for the righteous man,
because he is inconvenient to us and opposes our actions;
he reproaches us for sins against the law,
and accuses us of sins against our training.
He professes to have knowledge of God,
and calls himself a child of the Lord.
He became to us a reproof of our thoughts;
the very sight of him is a burden to us,
because his manner of life is unlike that of others,
and his ways are strange.
We are considered by him as something base,
and he avoids our ways as unclean;
he calls the last end of the righteous happy,
and boasts that God is his father.
Let us see if his words are true,
and let us test what will happen at the end of his life;
for if the righteous man is God's son, he will help him,
and will deliver him from the hand of his adversaries.
Let us test him with insult and torture,
that we may find out how gentle he is,
and make trial of his forbearance.

Let us condemn him to a shameful death,
for, according to what he says, he will be protected."

Exaltation of the just one (Wisdom 5:1-7)

Then the righteous man will stand with great confidence
in the presence of those who have afflicted him,
and those who make light of his labors.
When they see him, they will be shaken with dreadful fear,
and they will be amazed at his unexpected salvation.
They will speak to one another in repentance,
and in anguish of spirit they will groan, and say,
"This is the man whom we once held in derision
and made a byword of reproach—we fools!
We thought that his life was madness
and that his end was without honor.
Why has he been numbered among the sons of God?
And why is his lot among the saints?
So it was we who strayed from the way of truth,
and the light of righteousness did not shine on us,
and the sun did not rise upon us.
We took our fill of the paths of lawlessness and destruction,
and we journeyed through trackless deserts,
but the way of the Lord we have not known."

If we did not know that these passages were written in the first-century B.C. we might well mistake them for a later Christian meditation on Christ, the crucified and risen Lord. Indeed, according to the Acts of the Apostles, the early Christians confessed Jesus to be *the* suffering and exalted Just One. Referring to the Passion story, Peter said to the Jews: "You denied the Holy and Righteous One, and asked for a murderer to be granted to you, and killed the Author of life, whom God raised from the dead" (Acts 3:14-15; compare similar statements by Stephen and Paul in 7:52 and 22:14).

It is not by chance that this confession of Jesus as the Just One occurs three times in the Acts, written by the Evangelist Luke. The theological understanding of Christ's death as a divine "must" was indeed further developed especially by Luke. According to Mark and Matthew, the centurion had exclaimed after the death of Jesus: "Truly this man was God's

Son!" If the Roman officer said so, he meant not more than that Jesus had been an extraordinary, godly man. For the first two Evangelists, however, the centurion's reaction was nothing less than a confession of faith: "truly this man was *the* Son of God!" According to Luke, the centurion said something else, namely: "Certainly this man was [just]!" (Luke 23:47). With this the Roman commander simply stated that Jesus had been innocent. In Luke's Passion story the same opinion had earlier been expressed by Pilate, Herod Antipas, and even by one of the two Jewish rebels crucified with Jesus (Luke 23:4, 14–16, 41). While the term "innocent" rightly interprets what the centurion may have said, the Evangelist probably wanted us to understand much more: "Certainly this man was *the* Just One!"

Luke did more than transmit the early Christian tradition. He combined the understanding of Christ as God's suffering Just One with the recognition that Christ is also the suffering and martyred prophet. There are striking parallels between Luke's account of Stephen's martyrdom and that of Jesus (compare Acts 7:54–60 with Luke 23:26–49). Nevertheless, Jesus is not depicted simply as the first Christian martyr, as the model for the martyr-church. Rather, the whole Lucan Passion narrative is a call to discipleship. Therefore, Simon of Cyrene is seized to carry the cross "behind Jesus" (Luke 23:26). Simon thus becomes the example of the disciple who follows Jesus' call to discipleship (9:23). Christ as God's suffering Just One and as the suffering prophet has authority to forgive sins and to give access to God's kingdom (23:34, 41–43). This power to forgive leads to the miracle of conversion. Contrary to Matthew's account, Luke describes the signs in connection with Jesus' death not primarily as cosmic phenomena but as existential ones: he tells about the change of heart and the turning to Jesus by one of the rebels (vv. 40–42). He records the onlookers beating their breasts as they returned from Golgotha (v. 48). Later, in the Acts of the Apostles, Luke gives us many accounts of the growing number of conversions which lead to joy, witness, and suffering.

God's Suffering Just One and the
Human Cry for Justice

This third early Christian understanding of Christ's death i.e., the existential significance, has the most challenging implications for the laity in ministry. Three of them are mentioned here briefly for further exploration.

A first implication starts from the fact that Jesus was innocently executed, not by an angry mob, but after two legal trials. The Jewish and the Roman legal systems led to a juridical murder. This is like a parable for much of what happens today. Most oppression in this world does not come from evil persons or evil intentions. The cry for justice of millions of oppressed is caused by structures and actions which are perfectly legal in the eyes of those who created them. Thus, the present political structures in the East and the West with their military build-up are created for safeguarding national security. They want to preserve law and order. The ruling party or the elected parliament legalizes them. Nevertheless, how terrible are the impacts of these legalized national security systems on the poor within the rich nations and on the weak nations in between the power blocs, such as Afghanistan or Central America! The same is true for the economic systems, which may be perfectly legal in the countries from which they originate, but which create human havoc among the powerless and ecological havoc on God's earth.

The juridical murder of Jesus is thus like a mirror which shows us what all of us are involved in, sometimes with the best intentions, yet often ignorant of repercussions and at times reluctant to know them. Caught in such legal but oppressive structures, the ministry of the laity cannot mean to examine critically our ethical behavior *within* these structures only. The political and economic systems themselves need to be scrutinized. Not that we can build God's kingdom on earth, but together with people of other faiths Christians are called to seek alternative structures which are less oppressive for the powerless and less destructive for the earth which has been entrusted to us.

A second implication comes from the fact that Christ, the suffering Just One, is recognized as a brother and helper by those who themselves suffer and are oppressed. This was true for the one rebel crucified at Jesus' right side. It is true today for many among the millions who cry for justice. A remarkable phenomenon of contemporary church history is the rapid growth of basic Christian communities in almost all continents. The majority of these communities consist of poor, powerless, victimized persons, among them many women and children, people at the underside of history. They come together to read the Bible from their own perspective, to share one anothers' sufferings and joys, to celebrate the Eucharist. From the fellowship thus created they regain strength for persevering in their cry and their struggle for justice.

If we want to grow in discipleship, we must learn from members of such basic Christian communities who Christ is. They can teach us that the biblical term "righteousness" really means "justice"—justice, in the first place, for the oppressed and, therefore, at least initially, judgment for the oppressors. In the last decades reflection and action with regard to the ministry of the laity has centered much on the vocation of leaders, of white-collar workers, professionals, people on the upper side of history. This is important and must continue. But the time has now come to seek communion with those who recognize in Christ, first of all, God's suffering Just One and who in their own suffering have come to know Christ better than we do.

The third implication of this view of Christ as the suffering Just One is the most difficult. From the cross Christ calls us into discipleship. To make God's justice his cause brought him to his Passion. If we make God's justice our cause, suffering will not be far. We will come into strange company as Jesus did when he died between two rebels. In legal structures which are oppressive for the powerless we will have to do illegal acts, learn to say "no," perhaps start a civil disobedience movement like the present sanctuary movement. All this we can do with the knowledge that there is a divine "must" of suffering for those who respond to the cry for justice. All this we can do with the expectation that prison doors will be opened, that a new creation is at hand.

In Georg Lemke's crucifixion print we are face to face with God's Just One who was killed by a juridical murder. We hear the cry of a person representing the millions of exploited people on the underside of history, people who would not feel at ease in our relatively affluent local churches and in conferences on the ministry of the laity, yet people who existentially know Christ much better than we do. Above all, we see Christ the crucified leaning down from the cross and calling us into costly discipleship.

3

The Human Need for Identity and Christ the Artist

Have you ever looked at night through a large telescope, becoming silent in awe as you discovered the limitless universe of constellations of stars, far beyond the limited horizon of your personal life, beyond our small planet earth, beyond even the marginal "constellation" of our sun? Did you ever explore the infinitely small world with the help of a good microscope, and were you overcome by the wonder of the powers and the beauty of shapes hidden in matter and in the most elemental forms of life? Perhaps you then ponder with the writer of Psalm 8: "What is [the human being], that [you are] mindful of him [or her]?" (Psalm 8:4).

Or, you may have given birth to a child or assisted when a boy or girl was born: apparently a totally vulnerable being, and yet with amazing powers of survival and growth. You may have watched the long and painful and wondrous development from a crying baby to a self-affirming person, reflecting about himself or herself, beginning to make choices and to shape the world. Then perhaps you remembered how the same writer continued his conversation with God:

> What is [the human being], that [you are] mindful
>   of him [or her] . . . ?
> Yet [you have] made [that being] little less than God. . . .
>   —vv. 4-5

The Greek translators of the Old Testament were shocked by this phrase and therefore translated: "You have made the human being little less than the angels." However, the original Hebrew clearly states "little less than God," and here we are faced with that great paradox and riddle of our lives. Who are we? A handful of dust, living for a short while on the small planet earth; yet at the same time a little less than God, the creator of the whole universe.

Who Are We?

This question is probably the most typical human query, distinguishing human life from the life of plants and animals. In different ways it can be heard today all around the world. Who are we women, whose identity has been suppressed for so long by male domination and one-sided masculine ways of doing things? Who are we Africans or we people of the Pacific islands whose cultural identity was partly destroyed by colonial powers and is now threatened by the commercial and military interests of the big nations? Who are we farmers, whose land, where our souls lie, is taken away by large companies of agribusiness? Who are we manual workers, whose work which gave us identity is gradually taken away by machines and automation? "Who am I?," which is the typically Western version of this human quest in our individualistic and yet standardized society. Personal and corporate identity can indeed not be taken for granted. It is an elusive reality. Our search for it leads us through many identity crises; yet as soon as persons or social groups give up that quest, they lose much of their humanity.

The most common way to gain identity is to affirm oneself "over against" other persons or groups. This becomes the source of much tension and confrontation: children who grow up over against their aging parents, men over against women, one nation against the other, people of different social classes, races, and cultures confronting one another. Even Christians play this over-against identity game: Christianity versus Islam, Protestants versus Roman Catholics, Eastern Orthodox versus Western confessions, conservative evangelicals versus mainline Protestants, laity versus clergy.

There is a deep human need for identity, but our present quest for it separates us and leads to war. Can a biblical perspective on who we are help us to find our identity in a uniting way, a way which leads to peace? How does Christ respond to this query about who we are?

Poems of the Divine Artist

A most meaningful response to the question about our human identity is given by the writer of the letter to the Ephesians: "We are God's *poiēma*, God's artifact and poem, created in Christ Jesus for good works" (see Ephesians 2:10). Our true identity lies therefore in the fact that God made us his artwork: sculptures molded out of living flesh, kinetic art which is to become active. And this identity given to us is to serve God's purpose, not works for the honor of our ego, but—as the passage from Ephesians specifies—"good works, which God prepared beforehand, that we should walk in them" (2:10). The whole way of our life is thus to become a poem which communicates something of the design which God envisioned for us and creation.

Usually we do not think of God or of Christ as an artist. The metaphor of the divine artist is not borrowed from writings of biblical exegetes and theologians, though it is deeply biblical and can throw new light on the ministry of the laity. The metaphor comes from a side remark in the correspondence of the great Dutch painter Vincent van Gogh. In 1888, two years before his untimely death, Vincent wrote a series of revealing letters to his young friend Emile Bernard, a French painter and poet who was just beginning to discover the Bible. This is how Vincent responded to his friend's discovery:

> It is a very good thing that you read the Bible. . . . Now there it is in full force . . . the artistic neurosis. For the study of Christ inevitably calls it forth.
>
> Christ lived serenely, *as a greater artist than all other artists,* despising marble and clay as well as color, working in living flesh. That is to say, this matchless artist, hardly to be conceived of by the obtuse instrument of our modern, nervous, stupefied

brains, made neither statues nor pictures nor books; he loudly
proclaimed that he made . . . *living men,* immortals.[1]

We do not know if Vincent had any particular New Testament passage in mind when he wrote these words. Was it the
scene of the resurrection of Lazarus which two months before
Vincent's death he had actually painted? More likely Vincent
thought of the many people on the streets of Galilee who had
been rejected—the lepers, for instance—to whom Jesus gave
health and dignity. Or Vincent saw before his eyes the woman
who through an infirmity had been bent over for eighteen
years. Jesus healed her through his word and touch. He made
her straight, and immediately she praised God (Luke
13:10–13). Innumerable times such bent-over women and men
appear in Vincent's drawings and paintings, people in whom
the artist's eyes discovered part of God's artwork of living
human beings with great dignity.

The metaphor of Christ the artist may also have been
inspired by the prologue to John's Gospel, where it is said of the
Logos, God's Word and Wisdom which later became incarnate
in Jesus Christ, "All things were made through him, and without him was not anything made that was made. In him was
life, and the life was the light of [humankind]" (John 1:3–4).

In the middle ages this passage about the life-creating Logos
had led sculptors and painters to portray Christ as the great
architect, stooping down with a pair of compasses in order to
design the world and to bring order out of chaos.[2] In minia-
tures of medieval manuscripts and in frescoes and sculptures of
the cathedrals, we see Christ envisioning and then shaping
with creative hands the animals and the human beings. For me
the most moving visual representation of Christ the artist
comes from the northern portal of the cathedral in Chartres.
There, on an arch, a thirteenth-century unknown sculptor has
made a series of sixteen sculptured reliefs with the story of creation. Contrary to what is often assumed, these reliefs do not
show God, the Creator, at work. They portray the pre-existent
Christ, the creative Logos. We see him with a majestic gesture
of his hand separating the heavens from the earth. In deep con-

centration, almost as if sleeping, the Logos plans for the day and the night. Then with agile hands he forms the sun and the disk of the moon. The further reliefs show the creation of plants and animals, the calling into being of the earthly paradise leading up to the supreme act of creation. Just as a great sculptor sees in the still untouched block of marble the already finished figure, so the creative Logos is portrayed as envisioning the human being (see reproduction in this chapter). It is not yet that final act of creation itself, which appears only on a subsequent relief. First the moment of creative inspiration is shown, when in thought the Logos sees already that mysterious being to be created, which still stands waiting behind Christ the artist, still almost inseparable from him.

When the sculptor of Chartres made that relief he must have thought of the solemn divine decision which the priestly writers of the first biblical creation account report as follows: "Then God said, 'Let us make [*adam*] (not the man Adam, but the Hebrew term *adam*, designating here generally the human being) in our image, after our likeness' " (Genesis 1:26). In the ancient church and still during the early Middle Ages artists never portrayed the invisible God, except sometimes through a hand reaching down from heaven. Also, the sculptor of Chartres has not shown us God the Creator but Christ, the Logos, who becomes the visible manifestation and creative agent of that solemn divine decision to shape a being which is to represent God in the midst of creation.

This is how we became God's *poiēma*, God's living artifact in Christ Jesus. And it is as such an image of God that we find our deepest identity.

Created in God's Image ("Imago Dei")

Throughout the centuries Jewish and Christian thinkers have attempted to discover what the *imago Dei*, our being created in God's image, means for our human identity and calling.[3]

Only three times does this fundamental affirmation occur in the Old Testament, and it is always in the priestly account of primal history. Besides the already quoted divine decision to create human persons in God's image, there is a passage in the genealogy of Adam which says that the human beings were created in God's "likeness" (Genesis 5:1–2). The third passage occurs in the conclusion of the priestly account of the flood, where God says to Noah:"Whoever sheds the blood of [a human being], by [a human being] shall his blood be shed; for God made [the human being] in his own image"(9:6). Only in an intertestamental wisdom book of the second century B.C., the book of Sirach, is this particular biblical affirmation taken up again: "[God] made [the human beings] in his own image" (Sirach 17:3).

The Hebrew terms for "image" (*zelem*) and "likeness" (*demūt*) are practically synonymous. The first is used for a statue, a sculpture, or engraving; in Greek it is translated as *eikōn,* from which the word"icon"is derived. The second term—"likeness"—is a more general and abstract designation for a copy which resembles the original. The priestly authors obviously struggled to express a new insight. They borrowed concepts from Mesopotamian creation myths and stammered in awe as they tried to express with different terms that peculiar characteristic which relates us to God and gives us our true human identity.

Usually the attention immediately concentrates on what we are created for, on the human task which is the consequence of the *imago Dei.* "God blessed them, and God said to them, 'Be fruitful and multiply . . .'" (Genesis 1:28). Exactly the same words of blessing and command occur after the creation of the animals in the sea and the air (1:22). The faculty of procreation is thus not seen as something uniquely human. Procreation forms part of God's blessing; it belongs to the good creation, but it is not directly related to the image of God. The specific consequence of our unique relationship with God, rather, appears in the command: "Fill the earth and subdue it, and have dominion" (1:28; see also v. 26). Also in the earlier quoted text from the intertestamental wisdom of Sirach the *imago Dei* is linked with the task of dominion over the earth and recognition of God's majesty:

"The Logos envisaging the human being," also known as "God creating the birds envisages Adam in his mind." Sculptured relief, Cathedral of Chartres, France, thirteenth century. Photo Houvet.

[God] endowed [the human beings] with strength like his own,
     and made them in his own image.
He placed the fear of them in all living beings,
     and granted them dominion over beasts and birds.
Their eyes saw [God's] glorious majesty
     and their ears heard the glory of [God's] voice.
                                                    —Sirach 17:3-4, 13

The verbs used in these texts—"to have dominion," "to
subdue"—are very strong, pointing to severe royal rule. The
priests have taken up and further developed a view of the
human vocation which we came to know already from preexilic wisdom literature: as the trustees of creation, the human
beings are now also seen as God's viceroys on earth, representing God's sovereignty in the world.

Looking back on human history, especially Caucasian history since the Renaissance and the Enlightenment, one
becomes painfully aware of how dangerous this biblical view
of our vocation can become. The poem "Reverse Creation"
with which this series of studies began, showed the danger in a
dramatic way: dominion became exploitation; the trustees
usurped the role of autocratic masters; the viceroys transformed themselves into Promethean sorcerers, playing with
split atoms and genetic codes. Is this the inevitable consequence of our identity as those who are created in God's
image?

How Does the "Imago Dei" Mark Our Being?

In the past we concentrated too one-sidedly on what we are
called to *do*, and this was sometimes also true of discussions on
the ministry of the laity. The only World Council of Churches
Assembly which devoted a whole section to the ministry of the
laity—that of Evanston, 1954—called it significantly "The
Laity: the Christian in His Vocation." Both in the preparatory
material and in the report of that section most attention is paid
to the theme of work and vocation. Especially with the influ-

ence of the Protestant work ethics our identity is related too one-sidely with our daily work, with what we produce. Of course, wherever daily work is still separated from Christian faith and Sunday worship, there it is good to reflect on "the other six days" (title of a book by Joseph C. McLelland on the Christian meaning of work and property [Toronto: Burns & MacEachern, 1959]). It is refreshing to hear a Christian layman exclaim, "Thank God, it's Monday!" and in this spirit begin another week's daily work (title of a book by William E. Diehl [Philadelphia: Fortress Press, 1982]). However, the quality and significance of that work on the weekdays will depend much on what happens on the seventh day, when even God "rested from all his work which he had done in creation" (Genesis 2:3). Unless we periodically restore our being, i.e., our true human identity, the work will soon deteriorate. The biblical affirmation that we are created in God's image indicates to us in the first place who we *are*. We are not primarily a *homo faber*, somebody who *does* something, but an *imago Dei*, somebody whose *being* refers to God and in whose very existence God is uniquely involved. The passages in Genesis about the image of God give us some hints about what this means.

First, it is remarkable that in two of the three Genesis passages the creation of humankind in God's image is immediately linked with our being created male and female. Notice the change from the singular into the plural in both Genesis 1:27 and 5:1-2. "God created [the human being (singular)] in his own image . . . male and female he created them [plural]." (Genesis 5 has similar wording.) There is diversity in our personal and social identities, but not a divisive, "over against one another" diversity. Our fundamental human identity is common to people of the two sexes, of all races, nations and cultures. It is constituted not by an opposition over against one another, but by a *vis-à-vis*, a complementary communion. We cannot find our true human identity alone, but only in a reciprocal relationship between different persons and different groups. Our humanity can grow only in co-humanity (*Mitmenschlichkeit*). Seen in this way, the human quest for identity becomes uniting and not separating, a way to peace and not to war. This obviously has important implications for the ministry of the laity. It calls for mutually trusting support groups within the fellowship of the church. It also gives us an expectant and open attitude toward people who are different from ourselves. It commits us to struggle for a human community across all frontiers.

A second observation leads us to the heart of the matter: The *vis-à-vis* of human beings *with* one another and *for* one another reflects an even more basic *vis-à-vis*, a more fundamental face to face. It was God's solemn decision to create men and women as God's partners. To these correspondent persons God addresses the Word. From these partners God hears the cries, the prayers, and the praise. In a learned study of the *imago Dei* passages within the context of similar ancient Near Eastern texts, an Old Testament scholar made the suggestion that originally the image of God referred to the erect stature of the human body. According to this hypothesis, God created us in this typically human upright position so that we might be able to look up toward heaven and stand face to face with God, our Creator. For twentieth-century readers this may sound very naive, but we are always in danger of spiritualizing the Old Testament. Whether the just-mentioned hypothesis is tenable or not, for the priestly authors the fundamental human identity and dignity come indeed from God's solemn initiative to create men and women as God's *vis-à-vis*, as the Creator's partners in an ongoing dialogue and the ongoing work of creation. We become human in so far as we remain face to face with God through worship. This has again deep implications for the ministry of the laity. How can we maintain in our busy life and work that inner silence which allows God's Word to speak to us? How will we in our hectic attempts *to do* God's work find time *to be* before God in prayer and meditation?

A third observation concerns the question of whether this human identity of being created according to God's image was later lost. On the basis of the account of Adam and Eve's disobedience in the Garden of Eden (Genesis 3), which is not part of the priestly account, Christian dogmatics later developed the doctrine of the Fall. It is therefore often affirmed that the *imago Dei* was lost or has at least been strongly distorted. According to the priestly writers, however, this was not the case. Even after the Flood men and women were seen as created in God's image. Hence, human blood was not allowed to be shed (9:6). Similarly in the genealogy of Adam it is expressly stated that the unique human identity has been passed on to the next generations (5:3). Even in Jesus' time the Jewish rabbis never affirmed that the image of God was once and for all lost due to Adam and Eve's disobedience. There was some discussion of how individual human beings could lose the *imago Dei* through their sin, but the rabbis continued to presuppose that the image of God was still present in their contemporaries. As a result, Rabbi Hillel, an older contemporary of Jesus, called bathing a good work because he saw in the human body the image of God. For the same reason believing Jews were allowed to paint everything except a human being, for in this case they would paint God's image and thus transgress the second of the Ten Commandments. Again one can see important implications for the ministry of the laity: every human being has dignity. Our ministry has much to do with the look in our eyes. Can we discern God's image not only in productive and healthy persons who arouse our natural sympathy, but also in all the bent-over people on the underside of history, those whom Vincent van Gogh portrayed?

Christ, God's Image Who Transforms Us

The early Christians read the Book of Genesis as a whole, without making distinctions between the priestly account and other sources. The passages about the *imago Dei* were therefore seen in the context of Adam and Eve's disobedience. In a difficult passage of the First Letter to the Corinthians the apostle Paul reflected about how this human disobedience and sinfulness has affected our identity as those created in God's image. He speaks about "the first Adam" who "was from the earth, a man of dust." Through him sin and death came into the world. Yet God sent "the man from heaven," "the last Adam," namely the crucified and risen Christ. Through him "all are made alive." And Paul concludes this argument with the sentence: "Just as we have borne the image [*eikōn*] of the man of dust, we shall also bear the image of [*eikōn*] of the man from heaven" (1 Corinthians 15:21–22, 45–49). According to Paul, the true *imago Dei* can thus no longer be recognized in the generations after Adam and Eve, but this image of God can be restored in us through Christ.

An early Christian hymn indeed affirmed about Christ: "He is the image [*eikōn*] of the invisible God, the first-born of all creation" (Colossians 1:15). However, this can be seen only with eyes of faith, and Paul believed that evil powers had "blinded the minds of the unbelievers, to keep them from seeing the light of the gospel of the glory of Christ, who is the [image, *eikōn*] of God" (2 Corinthians 4:4). This affirmation has parallels in the postexilic wisdom literature, where a hymn to Dame Wisdom proclaims:

> She is a reflection of eternal light,
> a spotless mirror of the working of God,
> and an image (*eikōn*) of his goodness.
> —Wisdom of Solomon 7:26

As the wisdom incarnate Christ also incarnates the image of God. Thus the Johannine Christ could say: "He who sees me sees him who sent me" (John 12:45; see also 14:9).

Some decades before the apostle Paul wrote his letters, the Jewish philosopher Philo of Alexandria had developed complicated speculations about the *imago Dei*. Paul may have known of them, but his interest was not a philosophical one. On the basis of the conviction that in the crucified and risen Christ the image of God had been revealed to those with eyes of faith, Paul concentrated on a question which remains crucial also for us today: How can the *imago Dei* be restored in us? How can we become transparent for God so that when people meet us, they somehow experience something of God's presence and God's purpose for this humanity and this cosmos? Let's look at a few passages for possible answers.

To the Christians in Rome Paul confidently wrote: "We know that in everything God works for good with those who love him, who are called according to his purpose. For those whom he [knew beforehand] he also [determined in advance] to be conformed to the image [eikōn] of his Son" (Romans 8:28–29). This text does not specify when and how this transformation into Christ's image happens. Paul only expresses the firm conviction that conformity to Christ is God's will and that therefore we shall be transformed.

A second passage, taken from the Letter to the Colossians, makes a strong appeal for a conscious change of behavior which has immediate personal and social-ethical implications:

> Do not lie to one another, seeing that you have put off the old [human being] with its practices and have put on the new [one], which is being renewed in knowledge after the image [eikōn] of its creator. Here there cannot be Greek and Jew, circumcised and uncircumcised, barbarian, Scythian, slave, free man, but Christ is all, and in all (Colossians 3:9–11).

Where the image of God is being restored, the quest for identity will no more be divisive. With its variously shaped identities people from among all races, social classes, and cultures will form a community with one another and for one another. They find their basic human identity as they are incorporated into Christ's body, a notion which is central for the letters to the Colossians and Ephesians.

By far the most revealing but also the most difficult passage comes from the Second Letter to the Corinthians. Paul had reminded his readers of the strange story from Exodus, when the Lord spoke with Moses on Mount Sinai. The reflection of God's glory on Moses' face was so strong that he had to put a veil over his face when he met with the Israelites (Exodus 34:29–35). In contrast to this scene Paul wrote a sentence so dense with meaning that only a paraphrase can capture something of the overtones in the original Greek text: "All of us stand with an unveiled face. We reflect like in a mirror (or: "we contemplate as through a mirror") the glory of the Lord. Thus we are being transfigured into his image (*eikōn*), from one degree of glory to another" (2 Corinthians 3:18). In this passage we are not called upon to do something. We are simply asked to be a mirror: Not a mirror for examining ourselves, our shortcomings or successes, but a mirror for God's glory. Then gradually a metamorphosis will happen. This is exactly the verb used in Greek (*metamorphoumetha*), the same verb which occurs also in the transfiguration story of the Gospels (see, e.g., Matthew 17:2).[4]

There is not a single practical guide how this metamorphosis into the image, the icon of God, can take place in each of our lives. Some may be helped by a way of meditation, a prayerful face to face with Christ. Others will rather seek the communion with Christ where he is suffering as the Just One among those who cry for justice. For still others that mysterious transformation may begin as they seek wisdom in the Gospel narratives, letting themselves be called into question and be guided by that man from Nazareth who again and again astonishes us. There is not a single practical guide. However, unless we let that metamorphosis happen in us, we will never find our deepest human identity, nor will we be ready for the ministry of the laity.

Van Gogh's Response to Christ the Artist

To conclude, we will once again return to Vincent van Gogh who gave us the clue for these reflections on Christ the artist,[5] even though he was not in everything a model Christian layman.

His life story is well known. The son of a stern Protestant pastor, he soon revolted against the hypocrisy of Christians. Yet before that, the young Vincent spent days and nights reading, copying and memorizing biblical stories and sayings of Jesus. Then, in 1880, he worked with a total commitment as an evangelist among the coal miners in the desolate region of the Borinage in Belgium. Like a modern Francis of Assisi he began to take the demands of Christ so seriously that literally he became a fool for Christ's sake—so much so that the directors of the board of evangelization had to dismiss him.

It was then that Vincent found his true vocation: that of an artist. Often one assumes that with the rejection of his father, the church institution, and the calling to be an evangelist, Vincent also rejected his Christian origins. This is only partly correct. True, in the more than eight hundred letters published by Vincent there is a watershed in 1880. While before that date his correspondence was full of biblical allusions, afterwards the letters describe what the painter saw—the contours and colors of people and landscapes in Holland, Belgium, and France. However, the spirit of Christ continued to mark the eye and heart of this passionate artist. He never was blinded by superficial beauty or shallow truths. He went to the poor and suffering outsiders. As Christ in his parables saw in everyday events parables of the kingdom, so Vincent discerned in the most common things and gestures what at the same time is deeply human and refers us to the new creation. He discovered what is beautiful in the apparently ugly. Thus, he became the painter of the transfiguration who shows the divine glory in the created nature, the hidden image and poem of God in ordinary people.

Vincent never painted the biblical transfiguration scene, for he maintained a great inner retention to represent the Christ who had deeply shaped him. When his young friend Emile Bernard suddenly began to paint pathetic biblical scenes, for instance, an "Adoration of Magi," Vincent became angry. Look at "those fat ecclesiastical frogs kneeling down as though in a fit of epilepsy, God knows how, and why!" he wrote mockingly and then went on to comment about the very ordinary people among whom Jesus was born and whom Rembrandt or Millet had painted very truthfully.

In 1888 Vincent himself painted "Christ with the angel in Gethsemane," but he immediately destroyed it. Only one Christ painted by him is known to us; two versions of a copy of "Pieta" by Delacroix (1889). A few months before his death

Vincent also painted a large canvas of the "Resurrection of Lazarus," made according to a detail of Rembrandt's etching of the
same biblical scene. However, where in Rembrandt's etching
stands Jesus with his life-giving gesture, Vincent painted the
sun. It would be wrong to say that Vincent simply replaced
Christ by the sun, but his inner restraint forbade him to fix by
paint that one great artist who makes living human beings.
Therefore, he only pointed to Christ by the symbol of the life-
giving sun.

This hesitancy to represent Christ is a healthy warning for
our reflection on Christ's ministry and ours. More important
than to speak about Christ and our vocation as God's people is
to *be* the laity in the world, face to face with God and face to
face with our fellow human beings.

One of the many paintings of the sower by Vincent van
Gogh can impress this on our minds and hearts. We are called
to do things, to accomplish the "good works which God prepared beforehand, that we should walk in them" (Ephesians
2:10). Often this means simply to do the work of a sower, who
may never see the harvest nor even know whether the seeds
germinate and grow. We are also called to be the field, well
labored to receive the seed. And we are called to be the seed
itself, prepared to die so that new life can grow. To be the laity
in ministry presupposes, indeed, the readiness to let a painful
metamorphosis happen in our lives, to expose ourselves to the
molding hands of the divine artist so that our self-seeking ego
is changed into a life which bears much fruit. Thus, our true
identity, that of the image of God, is restored and in moments
of grace we may become for others icons of God's glory. All
this cannot happen by our own efforts but only through the
transfiguring power of Christ.

In him we find the source of true wisdom. His justice shines
from the cross like the sun. He is the artist who shapes us into
God's artwork.

4

For Building Up the Body of Christ

A Bible Study on Ephesians 4:1-16[1]

> He has the whole world in his hand,
> He has the whole world in his hand.

Our singing of this famous spiritual has led us right into the heart of this Bible study. Not only the *content* of what we sang, namely, God's universal power and care, relates to the core of the meditations and exhortations found in Ephesians 4:1-16,[2] but also the fact that we *sang* this message of faith corresponds to the way in which theology is communicated in that particular part of the New Testament.

A Song and a Secret

The author of the letter to the Ephesians—either Paul in his old age during a captivity in Rome or a disciple of Paul—encourages singing. Chanting and singing are, in fact, one of the oldest ways of memorizing and communicating biblical stories and affirmations of faith. The Christians who received this letter are encouraged to be filled with the Spirit and to address one another "in psalms and hymns and spiritual songs, singing and making melody to the Lord with all your heart" (Ephesians 5:19). There are direct and indirect allusions to the exaltation of Christ, the Spirit, and baptism. The meditations and exhortations contained in Ephesians may therefore be based on a baptismal service or a liturgical renewal of the bap-

tismal covenant during the Pentecostal period. They include
also the famous early Christian baptismal hymn:

> "Awake, O sleeper, and arise from the dead,
> and Christ shall give you light."
>
> —5:14

The language throughout the letter is marked by "liturgical
anticipations," hymnic confessions of faith which dare to
affirm the reality of the world not as it is experienced in human
everyday life but as it is believed to become according to the
secret plan of God.

The hymns and confessions of Ephesians reveal this secret
plan. What did God want to accomplish through Christ for the
universe (an ever-recurring term in Ephesians is *ta panta* =
"the all," "the universe")? What role does Christ's church have
to play in this secret plan?

A long and very involved sentence gives us the key for
answering these questions: *"[God] has made known to us in all
wisdom and insight the mystery of his will, according to his
purpose which he set forth in Christ as a plan for the fulness of
time, to unite all things in him, things in heaven and things on
earth"* (1:9–10); other translations render this secret plan as
follows:

> . . . that he would bring everything together under Christ,
>   as head,
>   everything in the heavens and everything on earth
>
> —*Jerusalem Bible;*

and ". . . that the universe, all in heaven and on earth, might be
brought into a unity in Christ" (NEB).

The church's task is to *know* this secret plan of God for the
universe and to prefigure that rich *unity* in Christ which God
intends for all. Therefore, the whole of Ephesians is one great
plea for unity. This plea is not only addressed to Christians in
Ephesus. The name "Ephesus" does, in fact, not appear in
some of the oldest manuscripts. Almost certainly "Ephesians"
was originally an encyclical with copies sent to various
churches in Asia Minor. The plea for unity is thus addressed to
all, including the Christians and churches today. No wonder

that this encyclical has become one of the most influential ecumenical documents.

In the fourth chapter the author challenges us to live up to our calling of unity (4:1–3). He concludes this exhortation by freely quoting an affirmation of faith which the early church perhaps used during baptismal services. Let us join into this confession!

First one side of the assembly addresses the other with the words of Ephesians 4:4–6; then this affirmation is recited by the addressees and finally all together confess:

> *There is one body and one Spirit,*
> *just as you/we were called to the one hope*
> *that belongs to your/our call,*
> *one Lord, one faith, one baptism,*
> *one God and Father/Parent of us all,*
> *who is above all and through all and in all.*

Building and Growing

The title of this Bible study—"Building Up the Body of Christ"—contains a strange combination of imagery: building is related to the growth of the body. There are many passages in the Old and New Testaments which speak about building, especially the building up of God's temple. In the New Testament are also many passages concerning the growth of the body. Only once in the Bible, however, in Ephesians 4:12, the combination of building and the growth of the body is found. It is part of one of the longest and most complicated sentences in the New Testament (in the original Greek Ephesians 4:7–16 forms one grammatical whole with interlocking affirmations).

In order to discover what the building up of the body of Christ means, I would like you to start with an ancient way of biblical understanding and communication. Put aside your printed Bible, for the Bible was originally not a book and certainly not printed on multicopied paper. It was originally an oral tradition: a story, with a lot of poetry and songs. One finds in the Bible more theo-poetry than theo-logy, more of the analogical and evocative language of poetry than the analytical and dissecting language of philosophy. In oral traditions symbols and gestures play an important role. Just as the prophets communicated not only through words but through prophetic acts, so Jesus blessed and embraced the children, cleansed the temple, washed the disciples' feet and broke the bread. Jesus knew that we think and understand not only with our brains but with our whole bodies. Let us, therefore, first use our hands for understanding something of that strange combination of building and growth imagery.

- —Make a "hand-mime" by which you build up your left hand so that it reaches up to God; use your right hand as a builder.
- —Then make a hand-mime in which both of your hands gradually grow up, reaching out towards God.
- —Finally, attempt to combine the building with the growth: let your left hand be built up and grow up towards God, and use your right hand as an enabler for building and growth.

After this exercise talk in buzz groups with your neighbors, teaching one another what you have learned about the building up of the body of Christ.

Reinterpreting the Gospel

The churches in Asia Minor to whom the encyclical of Ephesians was first addressed were deeply divided. Christians from among the Jews probably felt superior to Christians coming from the Gentiles in Asia Minor. At the same time these Jewish Christians were excluded from the synagogues and therefore felt at home neither among Jews nor among Gentile Christians. The Gentile Christians were confused and torn apart by the many religious philosophies which had a strong influence in Asia Minor. Therefore, the author of the letter made his plea for unity. In the second chapter he had addressed Gentile and Jewish Christians by explaining to them the Christian meaning of a prophetic passage, Isaiah 57:19, which he freely quoted. He showed how the dividing wall of hostility was broken down by Christ, who is our peace, and how those who were far off and those who were near became together fellow citizens and members of God's household (Ephesians 2:11-22). The fourth chapter again starts with this plea for unity, emphasizing one Lord, one faith, and one baptism.

However, this unity must not be mistaken for uniformity. The author therefore insists that *"Grace was given to each of us according to the measure of Christ's gift"* (4:7, emphasis added).

Before continuing his teaching about how the church is to minister and how it is thus being built up as the body of Christ, the author makes an excursus. He reminds the Christians who this Christ is, this giver of gifts, and what he has accomplished (4:8-10). Earlier, Paul or a disciple of Paul already had rejected false teachings among Christians in Colossae, a city of Asia Minor. The insights gained during that confrontation are taken up and deepened in the meditations in Ephesians about the mystery of God's plan. In Asia Minor of that time teachers of different religious-philosophical beliefs met and sought adherents: itinerant preachers of the popular philosophy of the Stoa (Stoics) who showed how God is in all things, in the whole universe; Jewish wisdom teachers with their cosmic speculations about how the world was created and how God's will was revealed, namely, through the personified Wisdom which was sometimes seen as the head of the body of this universe; Jewish sectarian missionaries propagating a spirituality like that of the Qumran community, teaching an ethical dualism and a spiritual warfare; early Gnostic believers emphasizing that salvation comes through knowledge (*gnosis*), the knowledge that the Redeemer, the perfect Man, has come to gather the souls of those who have true knowledge in order to save them out of this evil world through reuniting them with him and ascending into the highest heaven.

In restating the gospel about Jesus Christ to the Christians in Asia Minor, the author used typically Pauline theology and terminology and concepts of the religious philosophies and spiritualities just mentioned. This can be observed throughout the encyclical, but especially in 4:1-16 and the excursus of verses 4-8. Believers were apparently in danger of expecting passively the salvation which Christ had wrought. Some were content with an individualistic, purely "spiritual" hope while disregarding and despising the earthly realities. In order to correct such one-sided beliefs, the author reinterpreted the Pauline tradition of faith by using the religious "slogans" of Asia Minor: God's secret plan is being accomplished by the fact that Christ has come down to this earth (= incarnation); having defeated the evil powers, Christ victoriously ascended far above all heavens (= resurrection/ascension). He therefore now fills and rules the whole universe, and he can give gifts. In a typical rabbinical fashion the author "proves" this by using an Aramaic paraphrase (Targum) of Psalm 68:18. In the Hebrew Old Testament this psalm refers to God. In the Aramaic paraphrase it is applied to Moses. The author of Ephesians recognizes Christ as the one who ascended.

Who Ministers to Whom?

In Ephesians 4:11-12 the author takes up the thought started in verse 7. He now singles out some of Christ's gifts to his church and states their purpose. On the basis of the original Greek text, biblical scholars are still uncertain as to how to translate and understand the first part of verse 12. It is revealing to compare the two differing translations (of verses 11 and 12) of the Revised Standard Version—that of the editions before 1971 (A) and that of the editions since 1971 (B):

A: *"His gifts were that some should be apostles, some prophets, some evangelists, some pastors and teachers, for the equipment of the saints, for the work of ministry, for building up the body of Christ."*

B: *"His gifts were that some should be apostles . . . to equip the saints for the work of ministry, for building up the body of Christ."*

—Try to visualize a local church which lives and ministers according to translation A and a local church which lives and ministers according to translation B.

—After a moment of individual study share your insights with your neighbors in buzz groups.

From a purely linguistic point of view both translations are possible. However, both the context and the change of the prepositions in the original Greek text make it probable that the second translation ("to equip the saints for the work of ministry") is the right one. Most modern translations in English and other languages do, in fact, adopt it, as the following examples show:

". . . in order to fit his people for the work of service" (Goodspeed);

". . . so that the saints together make a unity in the work of service" (*Jerusalem Bible*);

". . . to prepare God's people for works of service" (NIV);

". . . to equip God's people for work in his service" (NEB);

". . . to prepare all God's people for the work of Christian service" (TEV).

If translation A of the Revised Standard Version is followed ("for the equipment of the saints, for the work of ministry"), it implies the following image of ministry of the church: in verse 7 both the words "grace" and "us" are then restricted to a set-apart group among the baptized, namely, the apostles, the prophets, and all others who received a special ministry within the church. *They* equip the "saints" (this is a common New Testament designation of God's people). *They* accomplish the work of ministry. *They* build up Christ's body. The work of ministry then belongs exclusively to these ministers, and the baptized remain more or less recipients only.

If, however, we follow the presently much more common translation B and its understanding, this will mean a Copernican change for many of us: *all* the members of the church have

received grace and are therefore called to service or—to say
exactly the same thing—called to ministry (the New Testament
uses only one word for "ministry" and "service," namely,
diakonia). This ministry of the church is entrusted to the
"saints," to such ordinary people as are most members of the
church. For this ministry of being a Christian in the world and
of together becoming ever more maturely the body of Christ,
we need to be trained, equipped, united, and strengthened.
The Greek word usually translated with "equipment" can refer
to the mending of nets, the ordering of a battle line, or, more
generally, the restoring, equipping, and joining together of
people for a task. It is for this purpose that Christ has given to
his church apostles and prophets, who laid the foundations,
and later also evangelists, pastors, and teachers. They form a
team of set-apart ministers. Not all their functions are concentrated in just one all-around minister or priest who is supposed
to do and know everything.

It is Christ who gives us such ministers. They are given so
that they might serve God's people in its ministry. It is not this
team who mobilizes the baptized for helping the ministers to
accomplish their task. One could almost say that the ministe-
rial team in Christ's army are, first of all, kitchen soldiers pro-
viding food for the fighting army. Some of them may also be
called to act as instructors in the barracks. From time to time
some may even be sent out as scouts on special errands. These
are extremely important functions and services in the fighting
army. The frontline soldiers, however, are Christian men and
women involved in the battles of faith in the midst of their
everyday life and work. For this they constantly need food,
strength, and that particular spirituality for resistance which is
described in the sixth chapter of Ephesians.

Such military imagery could easily mislead us. According to
Ephesians the church is not called to a crusade, for attacking
this or that evil or for changing the structures of society. It is,
first of all, called to *be* Christ's church, to stand firm and not
yield when the world's powers and principalities attack
(6:10–18). The baptized are called to bear one another's bur-

dens, oddities, and weaknesses so that all may walk together in unity. In this way the body of Christ is being built up.

The Purpose of It All

Ephesians 4:13–16 is the end of the long sentence which started in verse 7. This complicated closing contains so many mixed metaphors that it defies the art of most translators and exegetes. It further describes the process of building up and growing. In verse 15 a daring affirmation is made which has escaped the attention of many readers and commentators.[3] It, too, can be translated and understood in two completely different ways:

A: *"Speaking/living the truth in love, we are to grow up in every way into him who is the head, into Christ."*

B: *"Speaking/living the truth in love, let us cause to grow everything into him who is the head, into Christ."*

In most English Bibles and commentaries the first translation is used. Several German and French Bibles and commentaries, however, indicate both translations, and some (e.g., the German *Jerusalem Bible*) prefer the second translation. From a linguistic point of view both are, in fact, possible. The verb "to grow" (*auxēsōmen*) can have both an intransitive meaning ("we Christians grow up into") and a transitive/causative meaning ("we Christians let grow or cause to grow something into"). What is translated with "everything" (*ta panta*) can indeed mean "in every way," but in other passages of Ephesians it usually means "the totality," the "universe."

—Describe the vocation of the church according to translation A.

—Describe the vocation of the church according to translation B.

—After a moment of individual reflection share your insights with your neighbors in buzz groups.

Christ is confessed to be the head and chief over all things (1:22), who is the process of filling everything totally (v. 23). On the basis of such affirmations one would expect as a logical conclusion that the universe now already is—or is in the process of becoming—the body of Christ. However, the author of Ephesians never makes this affirmation. What he emphatically states is the fact that God has given Christ, the head over all, to the church, which is Christ's body. Two metaphors are therefore juxtaposed and kept in tension: Christ as the head over all and the church as the body of that head.

This same tension appears in the two possible translations of Ephesians 4:15, previously quoted. Because the church is confessed to be the body of Christ, it therefore must grow up in every way into him who is the head (translation A). However, this same Christ is the head of the universe; therefore, the church must become instrumental in everything growing into him who is the head (translation B). How is this to happen? What does Ephesians teach us about the church's mission in and for this world?

Some commentators believe that in Ephesians the "not yet" of the present world has almost totally been swallowed up in the "already" of the fulfilled hope. According to them, the church, therefore, has no mission except to worship God, to grow into the maturity of Christ—as is boldly stated in Ephesians 2:6—"to sit with Christ in heavenly places." It is indeed true that many passages of Ephesians are strongly marked by such a liturgical anticipation of the things to come. However, the second part of this encyclical consists of exhortations to the Christians: They must become what they are already in the sight of God! Although Christ has already begun to fill the universe, the struggle is still on, and Christians need to grow in spiritual resistance to evil forces.

A second group of interpreters solves the above-mentioned tension by saying that in the process of building up, ever new members and new areas of the universe will be incorporated into Christ's body. The whole universe is potentially now already Christ's body and will actually become the body of

Christ through the life and witness of the church. While isolated texts in Ephesians might suggest such a dynamic, expanding, and triumphal view of the church's mission (e.g., 3:10), this second interpretation hardly corresponds to the main message of the encyclical. The church's presence in the world is not envisaged as a crusade but as a *diakonia*, a service. The "military" passage in 6:10–18 does not portray a church which attacks and conquers. The armor given remains purely defensive: no bow and arrows, no spear, not even a battle sword. The "sword of the Spirit" is indeed not the long battle sword (*romphaia*) for attack but the short sword or dagger (*machaira*), handy for defense.

Neither a disinterested withdrawal from the world nor a conquering attitude toward the world characterizes the church in Ephesians. The two possible meanings of Ephesians 4:15 rather point to the fact that it is the church's worshiping and serving presence in the world which unmasks the evil powers and brings light into darkness. Before quoting the earlier mentioned baptismal hymn, the author wrote: "Since you have become the Lord's people, you are in the light. So you must live like people who belong to the light, for it is the light that brings a rich harvest of every kind of goodness, righteousness and truth" (5:8, TEV). Ephesians thus gives us two essential criteria with which we can measure the health and authenticity of each local and national church as well as that of the whole ecumenical movement:

1. The church is not an aim in itself. God's economy of salvation reaches out far beyond the world of Christians, even beyond the human world. It aims at filling the whole universe with divine glory.

2. The church must not lose its essential calling. This consists not in frantic activities to change the world. Rather, its calling is to *be* Christ's body in worship and everyday life. Its greatest service to the world is indeed to be a united church, growing up in everything into Christ, its head. Thus it becomes instrumental that everything may grow up into Christ, the head of the universe.

Notes

Chapter 1

¹For a good summary of how terms like "laity," "clergy/minister," and "ministry" were used in the laity discussions of the 1950s and 1960s and how the ministry of the laity was then understood, see the paper submitted by the World Council of Churches (WCC) Department on the Laity to the Fourth World Conference on Faith and Order at Montreal in 1963, entitled "Christ's Ministry Through His Whole Church and Its Ministers," English version published in *Encounter*, vol. 25, no. 1 (Winter 1964), pp. 105–129. For recent contributions and information about the ministry of the laity, see George Peck and John S. Hoffman, eds., *The Laity in Ministry* (Valley Forge: Judson Press, 1984), as well as the periodically published *Laity Exchange*, edited by Mark Gibbs for the Audenshaw Project (London, England) and the Vesper Society (San Leandro, California).

To see the term "laity" from the biblical concept of the *laos* (God's people) is theologically significant but both linguistically and historically wrong. This was already suggested by Ignatius de la Potterie's "L'origine et le sens primitif du mot 'laïc,' " in *Nouvelle Revue Théologique*, vol. 80, no. 8 (1958), pp. 840–853. See now the scholarly study on the development of a "laity" in the early church by the French historian Alexandre Faivre, *Les laïcs aux origines de l'Eglise* (Paris: Centurion, 1984).

²Throughout this book the Bible is quoted according to the Revised Standard Version. Only where needed, a more literal translation is made from the original Hebrew and Greek text. An attempt was made to use inclusive language, though in Bible quotations the masculine references to God ("he"/"his") have been maintained. This should not be understood as if God were a man. While more masculine references predominate, the Bible also includes important feminine references to God, as will be shown in the comments on the postexilic wisdom literature. God obviously transcends all such masculine and feminine metaphors. A good text to observe this is Hosea 11. There God is shown as a loving parent, a teacher, a healer, a farmer, a nurse, and a judge who repents from rightful anger, leading up to the self-affirmation in verse 9: "For I am God and not man [here the Hebrew term *isch* is used which does not designate generally the human being, but indeed the man], the Holy One in your midst."

³A song by Bernard Backman, from the record *Portrait of Man*, Mandala Productions, St. Paul, Minn., 1969.

⁴A very readable study on Old Testament wisdom literature and some of its implica-

tions for present church life is Walter Brueggeman's *In Man We Trust: The Neglected Side of Biblical Faith* (Atlanta, Ga.: John Knox Press, 1972). It includes an annotated bibliography on "Recent Study in Wisdom Traditions," pp. 132–138. There are much fewer New Testament studies on wisdom and Christ the sage. Compare especially P.E. Bonnard, *La Sagesse en personne annoncée et venue: Jésus Christ* (Paris: Cerf, 1966).

[5]Rosemary Houghton, *There Is Hope for a Tree,* a Study Paper on the Emerging Church. Multicopied paper, 1980, pp. 12ff.

[6]Alexandre Faivre, in *Les laïcs aux origines* has shown that in the primitive church of the first two centuries neither "clergy" nor "laity" existed. When at the end of the second century a group of believers began to be called "the laity," only baptized *men* who were husbands of one wife belonged to this group. Women could be appointed for certain ministries within the church, e.g., the recognized "widows," deaconesses, and later nuns, but they did not belong to the "laity" because at that time the group of the laity was not identical with the faithful in general. This continued to be so up to the fourth century when for the first time the term "laity" was generally applied to the faithful and began to include women also. See pp. 22ff., 70ff., 125ff., 234ff., 252ff.

Chapter 2

[1]The following information and hypotheses concerning the event and the earliest interpretations of the crucifixion of Jesus are based on my report on the research project about *Kreuz and Kultur:* Deutungen der Kreuzigung Jesu im neutestamentlichen Kulturraum und in Kulturen der Gegenwart (Mémoire de l'Institut des Sciences Bibliques de l'Université de Lausanne), Lausanne/Geneva, 1975, pp. 1–118 and notes on pp. 235–331. An English translation of the exegetical chapters of this report without the annotations was published under the title *The Cross: Tradition and Interpretation* (London: SPCK, 1979).

[2]The crucifixion print by Georg Lemke was published together with other prints by the same artist in the small volume of African prayers edited by Fritz Pawelzik, *Ich liege auf meiner Matte und bete* (Wuppertal: Aussaat Verlag, 1960), p.35.

[3]The drawings are made on the basis of the photographs and sketches published by J. Briend, "La Sépulture d'un Crucifié," in *Bible et Terre Sainte,* vol. 133 (1971), pp. 6–10. The first scientific reports about this archeological discovery were published by V. Tzaferis, J. Naveh, and N. Haas in the *Israel Exploration Journal,* vol. 20 (1970),pp.18–59. The debate about this discovery is still continuing among Jewish and Christian archeologists, historians, and theologians.

Chapter 3

[1]Vincent van Gogh, *The Complete Letters of Vincent van Gogh,* 2nd ed. (Boston: New York Graphic Society Books, 1978), vol. 3, pp. 495f.

[2]For a discussion of the creative Logos-Christ in medieval art, see the chapter "Der schöpferische Logos" in Paulus Hinz, *Deus Homo* (Berlin: E.V.A., 1981), vol. 2, pp. 88–95 and plates 178–186. The sculpture of Chartres on the Logos imagining the human being to be created is reproduced in my book *Immanuel: The Coming of Jesus in Art and the Bible* (Grand Rapids, Mich.: Wm. B. Eerdmans Publishing Co., 1984) plate 32.

[3]On the biblical *imago Dei* passages see Ludwig Köhler, "Die Grundstelle der Imago-Dei-Lehre, Gen. 1,26" in *Theologische Zeitschrift,* vol. 4 (1948), pp. 16–22; Friedrich

Horst, "Face to Face: The Biblical Doctrine of the Image of God," in *Interpretation*, vol. 4, no. 3 (1950), pp. 259-270; an analysis of the term *eikōn* by Gerhard von Rad, Hermann Kleinknecht, and Gerhard Kittel, in *Theological Dictionary of the New Testament*, ed., Gerhard Kittel and Gerhard Friedrich (Grand Rapids, Mich.: Wm. B. Eerdmans Publishing Co., 1964), pp. 381-397.

⁴There remains a last *imago Dei* passage in the New Testament which is highly embarrassing for modern readers. In his ill-famed excursus about the veil necessary for women in Christian worship Paul wrote: "A man ought not to cover his head, since he is the image [*eikōn*] and glory of God; but woman is the glory of man" (1 Corinthians 11:7). In a typically rabbinic fashion Paul argues that the woman was created after the man (Genesis 2:21-23) and that she has therefore not the character of an image of God (1:26-27) but is only a reflection, a "glory," of that image. In the context of the whole passage of 1 Corinthians 11:1-16 this scriptural reasoning is used to "maintain traditions" and the "practice" of the churches in Paul's time (vv. 2 and 16), based on what then was considered to be "dishonoring," "disgraceful," and "degrading," or, on the contrary, "proper" and in accordance with what "nature itself teaches" (vv. 5, 6, 13, 14). Clearly there is here no commandment of Christ. Paul only safeguards a Jewish custom. Besides his hardly convincing reasoning from Scripture and from nature, Paul also refers to an "authority" on the woman's head, namely, "because of the angels" (v. 10). Though many scholars have attempted to interpret this obscure text, its meaning will probably never be fully clarified. Perhaps it alludes to Genesis 6:1-4 and points to the threat of angelic powers for women who pray and prophesy in spiritual enthusiasm. Or does this text suggest that when women pray and prophesy in the Christian assembly, the order of this creation is superseded in the presence of angels by the order of the world to come? In this case the veil would be a sign of authorization received from God. Whatever the meaning of this passage may be, in verse 11 Paul acknowledges that "in the Lord" men and women are mutually partners, reciprocally dependent on each other.

⁵The best analysis of all Vincent van Gogh's paintings and drawings in the light of his letters is the large volume by Jan Hulsker, *Van Gogh en zijn weg: Al zijn tekeningen en schilderijen in hun samenhang en ontwikkeling* (Amsterdam: Meulenhoff, 1977). For the paintings referred to above, see pp. 408ff., 448, and 485, as well as the earlier mentioned correspondence with Emile Bernard, letters B8, 9, 19, and 21.

Chapter 4

¹This Bible study on Ephesians 4 was conducted at the meeting of the World Council of Churches' Unit III on Education and Renewal with representatives from North American churches, Atlanta, Georgia, April 1985.

²The most detailed commentaries on Ephesians are the two volumes by Markus Barth, *Ephesians,* The Anchor Bible (Garden City, N.Y.: Doubleday & Co., Inc., 1974), vols. 34 and 34A. The following Bible study is based on my larger study on Ephesians, *A Plea for Unity,* cassette and worksheets, WCC, Geneva 1980.

³For the interpretation of Ephesians 4:15 see especially Petr Pokorny, *Der Epheserbrief und die Gnosis,* (Berlin: E.V.A., 1965), pp. 65-81; and R. P. Meyer, *Kirche und Mission im Epheserbrief* (Stuttgart: Kath. Bibelwerk, 1977).